Davy the Punk

A life so fascinating, hilarious and outrageous, it's worthy of a Mordecai Richler novel. — Andreas Schroeder, author of *Renovating Heaven*

Davy the Punk spins his tales tall and true to the circle of Jewish hoods in 1940s Toronto, mesmerizing them and us. In this memoir of a childhood that is the stuff of dreams and movies, Bob Bossin pays loving tribute to a father whose name alone conjures up a lost world. With a songwriter's ear, a performer's sense of timing and a poet's grace, he brings that world back to life. The apple (or, in this case, the apple strudel) doesn't fall far from the tree. — Si Kahn, author, musician and organizer

I loved this. This generation [Bossin] writes about has now vanished, but the colourful, hard-talking comedic experience of life on the edge comes back. Bossin is a great storyteller, and these are great stories. I can hear the voice of that generation clearly. Wonderful! — Clayton Ruby, lawyer

Bob Bossin's father Davy lived in the seamy underside of Toronto the Good between the wars—a Runyonesque milieu of bookies and baseball, horses and payoffs, right in the zone where crime buys a drink for enterprise. Bossin's memoir of Davy is fascinating, funny, dark and poignant —a vividly readable portrait of an unforgettable man in a remarkable habitat. — Silver Donald Cameron, author of *The Living Beach*

Davy the Punk is a thoroughly enjoyable and revealing romp through the historical underside of Toronto the Good. With verve and enthusiasm, Bob Bossin brings a performer's skill to the tall but true tales in what is, ultimately, his family's story. — Lilian Nattel, author of *Web of Angels*

Amid the fascinating and sometimes belly-laugh-funny anecdotes of underworld life in mid-20th-century Toronto the Good, *Davy The Punk* depicts a son's poignant search for his infinitely resourceful, elusive and wounded father. Bob Bossin has penned a witty and generous memorial to a man, we sense, he is still seeking to know.
— Gabor Maté M.D., author of *In The Realm of Hungry Ghosts*

DAVY THE PUNK

BOB BOSSIN

The Porcupine's Quill

Library and Archives Canada Cataloguing in Publication

Bossin, Bob, 1946–, author
 Davy the punk / Bob Bossin.

ISBN: 978-0-88984-369-1 (pbk.)

 1. Bossin, Bob, 1946–. 2. Bossin, Davy. 3. Folk singers—
Canada—Biography. 4. Bookmakers (Gambling)—Canada—
Biography. 5. Fathers and sons—Canada—Biography. I. Title.

ML420.B68A3 2014 782.421620092 C2014-900192-4

Published by The Porcupine's Quill, 68 Main Street, PO Box 160,
Erin, Ontario NOB 1TO. http://porcupinesquill.ca

Readied for the press by Doris Cowan.

Represented in Canada by Canadian Manda.
Trade orders are available from University of Toronto Press.

We acknowledge the support of the Ontario Arts Council and the Canada Council
for the Arts for our publishing program. The financial support of the Government
of Canada through the Canada Book Fund and the Government of Ontario
through the Ontario Media Development Corporation is also gratefully
acknowledged.

Canada

Ontario
Ontario Media Development
Corporation

Canada Council Conseil des Arts
for the Arts du Canada

ONTARIO ARTS COUNCIL
CONSEIL DES ARTS DE L'ONTARIO

For Davy and Marci,

and for Davy and Gee

• Table of Contents •

'Is that true?'

'It's a true story.'

'It really happened?'

'It's a true story.'

— A.J.P. Froehlich

1. The best way to not get hit by a baseball •

IT IS THE SUMMER of 1956 and I am sitting with my father, Davy Bossin, in the bleachers above first base in Maple Leaf Stadium, the old ballpark on the shore of Lake Ontario. Summer nights in Toronto are as humid as a Georgia swamp, and the stadium on the waterfront has been dubbed 'the poor man's air conditioning'. Davy is sitting in the comforting breeze off the lake, reading the newspaper. I am giving him a fervent play-by-play of the game between the Maple Leafs and the Havana Sugar Kings. I am ten.

Through the early innings, we are joined by one, then another of my father's cronies, who gather in the evening air to swap stories, argue politics, and only incidentally watch baseball. By my father's decree, my colour commentary stops when the friends show up. This is fine with me; I love hearing the men talk the way they do when they are away from their work and their wives. I make myself as small as I can, hoping that my presence will be forgotten and I will overhear some secret that would otherwise be withheld until I have been dispatched for peanuts or hot dogs. Toronto was known, in those days, as Toronto the Good, but the Toronto these men know is tantalizingly bad.

'Did you see Benny Kaufman died?'

'Benny the Shoykhet? With the book in the little butcher shop in the alley off Kensington?'

'Yeah, exactly. Benny's gone, *alev ha-sholem*.'

'Did he ever get pinched? I don't think he ever got pinched. He had a hell of an operation. You could make a bet, have a drink and buy a chicken.'

'Did he actually sell chickens?'

'Sure he did. They were good kosher chickens. Of course he always kept a few in the back in case of a raid. He had one of the kids out at the street, who'd whistle if the cop turned into the alley. Then the *bubba* would come downstairs and they'd stick the bottles in her apron and throw a couple chickens on top, and she'd shuffle down the alley, smiling and nodding at the cop. Benny stuffed his betting slips up the ass of one of the chickens. They never caught him.'

'Yeah, they did. Herbie Thurston pinched him. Remember, Harry Thurston's boy who became a cop.'

'Nah, you're all mixed up. Herbie never pinched Benny; the guy he pinched was Murray the Rug.'

'In the old dry cleaner's on Dovercourt!'

'Exactly. When he was a kid, Herbie used to go in with his father, when the old man placed his bets. Then when he became a cop, he went to Murray, and he told him, "Murray, I'm a policeman now and I'll arrest you if I have to. You've done well, it's time you retired." Of course Murray didn't listen. He looked at Herbie, and saw the little *pisher* tagging after his old man. And nobody had ever been able to charge him, because they could never find his slips. But Herbie knew from his father that Murray kept them under his toupee. So he nailed him.'

The stories go back and forth, of this bookie who got busted, of that one who never did. My father sits there reading the paper. The conversation flows by him, like water around a rock.

'What was the name of the guy ... the one they arrested over and over?'

Silence. Nobody remembers. Then a new voice says, 'Shnooky Schneider. It was Shnooky Schneider.' The voice is my father's.

When Davy speaks, it is as if he were a king. Heads turn. This is because he speaks so rarely. And because, when he does, he is a natural-born story-teller. He folds his paper, none too quickly, and begins to recount how Arnie the Shnook Schneider was busted for bookmaking sixty-seven times, every one a first offence.

'In those days Arnie was working for Manny Feder,' my father begins quietly, 'back when Manny and his brothers had the big horse room on Queen Street, before they opened the Brown Derby. It was a pretty smooth operation, as it oughta be, since Manny had half the cops in town on the pad.

'But every now and then, the heat would be on. Old Reverend Domm would get up in Bathurst Street Church and preach a fire-and-brimstone sermon on vice, and then Holy Joe Atkinson would publish the whole damn thing in the *Star*: "Sunday morning, in Bathurst Street United Church, the Reverend Gordon Domm warned of the wave of corruption loosed on the city by gambling racketeers."'

My father gives the *Star* the voice of Walter Winchell. As the plot heats up, so does his delivery.

'Then the next day they'd send some cub reporter down Queen Street to lay some bets at some of the bookie joints, as if that was news to anybody, and they'd run that on the front page. And that would get the Decent Citizens riled up, and they'd start demanding that the police *do* something.

'So the cops would call Manny and say, "Sorry, Mr Feder, but we're gonna have to raid." And they'd tell him when. Then Manny would call Shnooky and tell him to get ready.'

Here my father pauses, pretending to some interest in what is happening on the field. The men around me wait for him to go on. It seems to me all Maple Leaf Stadium does.

'Manny's joint was on the second floor and it would be going full blast with punters betting, smoking their cigars, the phone ringing, odds coming in and getting chalked up, the loudspeaker blaring—"They're at the post. And they're off ...".

'But upstairs, on the third floor, there was another room with just a table, an unconnected phone and a folding chair. And that's where Shnooky would wait for the cops. They'd come charging in, up the stairs, past the horse room, straight to the third floor. They'd arrest Shnooky and grab the telephone, so they could report that "gambling equipment was seized". Then they'd go back downstairs, past the horse room again, and take Shnooky to the station, where Manny would be waiting with Shnooky's bail. Then, when Shnooky was convicted, Manny would pay the fine, which was, by standing agreement, a hundred bucks. It was like a tax.

'Of course the law said that, on a third conviction, bookmakers go to

jail. But the cops would misplace Shnooky's priors, or the magistrate would be one of Manny's customers, or both. So every time, it went down as Shnooky's first offence. And the government got its hundred bucks, which was good money in those days.'

Sometimes the laughter from our section was so raucous the pitcher would turn and look up.

MY FATHER DIED in 1963. I had just turned seventeen. The funeral filled Holy Blossom Temple, which surprised the hell out of me. Davy was not exactly a friendly guy. Away from his pals at the ballpark, he hardly said two words to anyone. And yet the pews were filled.

'Your father was very shy,' somebody told me, which wasn't true. Someone said, 'Davy liked horses better than people'—but that wasn't so either. He merely knew, and he made sure I knew, that what you don't say can't be used against you.

I grew up knowing a little about Davy's 'life of crime': that he wasn't a bookie but, in my mother's phrase, 'a bookies' bookie'. I knew that there had been a precedent-setting court case, but by the time I wanted to know the details, he was gone. He was not a man who kept a diary, and though he told terrific stories, the stories were never about himself. Of course they were *all* about himself, which may be why I hung on every word.

Over the years, I have unearthed whatever I could about my father, and pored over the shards like an archaeologist. But there is only so much the shards can tell you, no matter how much you brush them and turn them around. The worst is, I can't help wondering what Davy would have told me if only I had asked him. *What did it teach you?* I want to know. *What would you have taught me when I was old enough?* I did ask him once if he had met Al Capone. He hadn't.

Davy was a good father in his own way. I remember, when I was ten, I suggested the two of us go to the movies on Friday nights, as a father-and-son thing. I loved movies. To my surprise, he agreed. One week I chose, and we saw *Forbidden Planet* or *Davy Crockett, King of the Wild Frontier*. The next week he chose, and I became the only kid in Allenby Public School to see *Cat on a Hot Tin Roof*.

So mine was not an entirely normal upbringing. But then, I was not a standard, Norman-Rockwell-type son, if there is such a thing. I think my father and I would both have liked to be, well, more normal, for each other's sake, but it wasn't in the cards. For my part, I was a poor athlete.

That was no small thing for a boy in the 1950s. My father tried teaching me to catch a baseball. It was painful for both of us. 'Getting hit by a baseball hurts,' he would shout to me across the grass. 'Joe DiMaggio said that. And the best way to not get hit is to catch it!' It didn't help. But we were back at it the next day.

A HALF-CENTURY LATER, on a crisp spring afternoon, I am at the ball field with my son, tossing a baseball. I tell him what Joe DiMaggio said. He says, 'Who's Joe DiMaggio?' We move on to batting. I tell him, Keep back. Hands in tight. Don't swoop. He says he *likes* to swoop. I know he is silently calculating how long it will be until he can get back to his Xbox. I want to tell him, 'Save *this*. Back it up and write protect it!' *One day, I want to say to him, you're going to want to remember this. One day you will wish you could remember even the smallest detail.*

But I don't say that. I say, 'Remember, push off your back foot.'

And he says, 'Can we stop now?'

'Yeah, that's enough for today.'

We head for the car, and I remind myself that ripeness is all.

'Hey, you hit some good ones today,' I tell him.

2. Sweet Lilies' advice • •

'Tom Stein had the biggest book in Alberta ...'

I CAN STILL HEAR my father's voice. We are at the Sea Hi Chinese
Restaurant on Dundas Street, in what was once the Ward, the Toronto
slum where my father grew up in the early years of the twentieth century.
Back then it was Toronto's Jewish ghetto, but by the 1950s the Jews had
moved west and north, and Dundas had become the heart of Chinatown.

That night, we sat at Davy's regular table with half a dozen of his pals.
Among them were my uncle Hye, Paul Grosney, the Winnipeg-born trum-
pet player, a long-faced horse player I called Mr Sniderman (everyone else
called him Sack), and at the end of the table, taking two places, Sam Shop-
sowicz. Shopsy was the biggest man I had ever seen, and the most famous.
A cartoon of his jowly face adorned every package of Shopsy's Hot Dogs
(it still does today, a half-century later). Shopsy had inherited his parents'
delicatessen in the mid-1940s, and, advertising himself as 'The Corned Beef
King', he turned it into the city's premier Jewish deli. He then started his
own meat-packing business, which he would eventually sell to Lever
Brothers, who would sell it to Maple Leaf Foods. Shopsy died young.
Looking back over that table, I realize most of them died young: my uncle
Hye, Sack Sniderman, and my father as well. But that night they were all
hale and happy, relaxed in each other's company, enjoying the Sea Hi's
familiar fare and, even more, enjoying the stories that went back and forth.
Particularly Davy's stories.

'... Stein had the biggest book west of Winnipeg. He was a tough guy
and he had done real well for himself out west. He even had his own string
of horses, including a big grey gelding named Peachstone. Peachstone was
a very fast horse. He won so often that, after a while, nobody in Alberta
would bet against him.

'So Stein ships Peachstone out to Vancouver. He figures, out there, he
can still get some action. He hires the best jockey—in those days that was
Scotty Craigmyle, hands down—and he enters Peachstone in the feature.
Then he sits back to watch the fun.

Scotty Craigmyle, mounted.

'But just before the race, Stein gets a call from back in Calgary. His book is way overloaded on Peachstone, and they can't lay any of it off because all the other bookies are swamped with bets on Peachstone too. If the horse comes in, Tom is in deep shit. So he jumps in a cab, rushes out to the track, and catches Scotty Craigmyle in the paddock. He grabs the halter, points a finger at Scotty, and says, "Under no condition can dis horse win dis race!"

'Meanwhile, they've called the horses to the starting gate. Scotty is try-ing to figure out what the hell to do. He knows he has to pull the horse, but how, without making it too obvious? All the way to the gate, he's thinking about it. Finally, with the race about to start, he decides he'll break Peachstone so fast, and push him so hard for the first half-mile, that he runs himself out.

'No sooner does he decide this than the bell clangs and the gates spring open. Scotty gives the horse the boot and Peachstone takes off like a bat out of hell. Then, sure enough, by the half-mile, Peachstone starts to flag. Another eighth and he's wheezing like an old squeeze box. Scotty sneaks a look over his shoulder, but what he sees is not good. The closest horse is ten lengths behind and dropping back like a fat cop chasing a schoolboy. None of the horses are gaining so much as a yard. That's when it hits Scotty that the other jockeys are all pulling their horses too. They had all bet on Peachstone!'

There my father pauses to take a bite of Sea Hi fried rice. Davy is very good at pauses. It is unclear whether he intends to go on. Eventually Shopsy says, 'Davy! So? What happened?' I suspect my father has been waiting for this.

'So,' Davy says, 'what happens is, Scotty does the only thing he can. He eases over to the rail, pretends to bump, and falls off the horse.'

The men roar. Grosney claps the tabletop. Even the taciturn Sack Sniderman's mouth twitches. Davy laughs as heartily as the rest. I think these men like nothing better in the world than sitting here, bullshitting with each other. Davy is in his element. At this table he is a star. I feel proud.

IF I COULD TIME-TRAVEL, it would be back to the Sea Hi that night, or another like it. I loved Davy's stories. I suppose it is because mostly he said nothing. When he did speak, he was gruff. But when he was with Shopsy, Sack Sniderman, and the others, Davy could run neck and neck in a field with Sam Levinson, Damon Runyon and Sholem Aleichem. At least that was so by the 1950s. By then he was legal, out of gambling and booking acts into supper clubs. It was a short walk from the gambling business to show business in those days. In the 1940s and '50s, much of the entertainment industry—clubs, agencies, record companies, even the Ed Sullivan Show, by some accounts—was underworld controlled or financed. The supper clubs were home turf to the hoods. On Saturdays, they brought their wives for dinner and a show. Fridays, they brought their mistresses.

Davy acquired his talent agency, Theatrical Attractions, as payment of a debt owed to him from his gambling days. Or so the story goes. He took readily to his new line of work. He had always loved shows—vaudeville, musicals, nightclubs. It was a taste he inherited from his father, Zussman Bossin. My grandfather, who was born in the Ukraine in 1866 and emigrated to Canada in 1904, was a righteous and stiff-necked Old World Jew, a pillar of Toronto's *russische shul*, yet every Friday night after *shabbes* dinner, Zussman rose from the table and walked to the Gaiety Theatre to catch the vaudeville show. He had struck a deal with the Gaiety: he displayed their playbill in the window of his junk store, and in return, they gave him a Friday-night ticket. Thus he could attend the show without touching money on the Sabbath.

Zussman cut an incongruous figure in the Gaiety's audience, sitting at the back with his beard, derby and gabardine coat, drumming his fingers to the band. In 1884, when he was a conscript in the Russian army, he had won a battalion-wide drumming competition. However, when the judges realized that he was a Jew, the prize was given to someone else. It was the only story from his army days my grandfather ever told.

MY FATHER'S OFFICE, Theatrical Attractions, was on the second floor of the Barclay, a threadbare hotel on Front Street, midway between Union Station and the ballpark. Its location and low monthly rates made it a favourite haunt for the underpaid players who made up the roster of the Toronto Maple Leafs. I would see them snoozing in the lobby's cracked leather armchairs. This made the Barclay one of the grand hotels in my ten-year-old's estimation. To grown-ups, the Barclay was the home of the Club Indigo, the city's hottest nightclub. The Indigo boasted its own band, its own chorus line, and a fresh headliner every week—booked by my father.

In the mid-1950s, the Barclay and the Club Indigo were owned by Al Siegel, who was said to be a cousin of Ben 'Bugsy' Siegel. Al was reputed to be 'connected'. Though my father booked the shows, he had as little to do with Siegel as possible. Most people did. But one time in the early 1960s, Joey Bishop came to town to headline a benefit for the Variety Club, the show business charity, on a Sunday night. At the last minute, trouble arose with the stagehands' union concerning overtime, and it looked like the show might be cancelled. Desperate, someone at the Variety Club called my uncle Hye, who was a member. Hye called Davy, who called Siegel, who called New York, and the union problem vanished. I watched the show from the wings with my father.

By then I was working for Davy Saturdays and holidays, helping out around the office. I have never understood why he hired me. The workload was non-existent. From time to time, I would be handed something to file, or sent to the hotel kitchen to pick up coffee. I suspect Davy just wanted to get me out of the house, or out of my mother's hair. Maybe he wanted me to learn a little about business. Or maybe, since he was not a demonstrative man, this was his way of being close.

So Davy and I would take the bus downtown to his office in the Barclay, where I would sit on the couch and listen while he hollered into the telephone, his preferred mode of negotiating. Once, a Montreal club owner refused Davy's offer of Lena Horne because, he said, 'We don't hire coloured girls.' Davy turned the air blue. Another time, Davy was auditioning a young black singer in an empty Toronto club, when the owner— another mobbed-up character—came in. 'Get that nigger out of my club!' he ordered. The singer was Harry Belafonte.

Davy was good at his job. He had an eye for talent and a head for figures, though he did not seem to work a lot harder than I did. Many of the afternoons at Theatrical Attractions were spent sitting around with the

Paul Grosney with Louis Armstrong

visiting acts, Sandman Sims, Mel Tormé or the Deep River Boys—whoever was in town with the afternoon to wile away. I loved those sessions, even if I have forgotten the stories they swapped. In fact the one time I remember clearly, my father told a story he made sure I didn't hear.

It was in the late '50s, just after Tommy Dorsey died. There were four or five men sitting around Davy's desk, including Davy's pal and the Club Indigo's band leader, Paul Grosney. The news of Dorsey's death was a shock. At fifty-one, Dorsey led the biggest big band in the business. He had choked in his sleep. 'Unless,' Grosney said, 'one of the musicians did it.'

'I wouldn't be surprised,' one of the others agreed. 'He was a mean, cheap bastard. Even his brother quit him.'

'I bet he made Jimmy buy himself out of the contract too.'

'Like Sinatra. You know that story?'

It was a rhetorical question. Paul Grosney had once played a gig with Dorsey and he relished telling the Sinatra story.

'When Frank was just starting out, he was singing in a carpet joint in Hoboken. Bugsy Siegel took a shine to him. Bugsy introduced Frank to Harry James, who signed him for $75 a week. Frank cut his first record with Harry, "All or Nothing at All". Things were really starting to roll for

Frank. Dorsey got wind of it. He checked Sinatra out and hired him away from Harry. Harry just let Frank go. He wasn't going to hold him back. Harry was that kind of a guy.

'But Dorsey—what a prick he was. He signed Sinatra for $150 a week and, in return, he made Frank sign over a third of his earnings for life, plus another 10 percent on top to Dorsey's agent. Talk about a rotten deal.

'Well, a couple years go by, and Frank does "I'll Never Smile Again". He does "Blue Skies", he does "Stardust". The kids love him. So he wants to go out on his own, but Dorsey won't let him out of the contract. Frank offered Dorsey $60,000 to let him go. Dorsey turned him down flat. So Frank went to see Bugsy. Siegel goes to Dorsey and hands him a paper with an offer to buy Sinatra's contract for a dollar. Then he takes out a gun and points it at Dorsey's head. "In one minute," he says, "either your signature or your brains will be on the paper."'

'That really happened?' somebody asked.

Everyone, including Grosney, turned to Davy.

Davy didn't say anything at first. Then he said, 'It wasn't Siegel, it was Willie Moretti. He grew up in Hoboken and knew Dolly, Frank's mother. If it had been Siegel, he would have whacked Dorsey around first and *then* got out the paper.'

'Yeah, Bugsy was a piece of work. And so was she.'

'Who, Sinatra's mom?'

'No. Virginia. Virginia Hill, Siegel's girl. What a dame. Davy knew her. Right, Davy?'

Davy didn't speak.

'Was she as beautiful as they say?' somebody said, filling in the silence, urging Davy along. Everybody was still looking at my father.

'Yeah,' Davy finally answered, 'she was a knock-out. And she had a head on her shoulders and a lot of moxie. She used to run layoff money between Chicago and New York.'

Then Davy noticed I was there, and stopped.

'Davy,' Grosney said, 'tell the story about her and Senator Kefauver.'

Davy looked at me, then at Grosney, then back at me. 'Bobby, go get some coffees.'

I took their orders and hurried downstairs to the Barclay's kitchen. I got the drinks in no time, put them on Davy's tab, and ran back upstairs to the office. The door was locked. I knocked. No one answered. Through the door, I heard the rumble of my father's voice. I knocked again. There

were no footsteps, just Davy's muffled words. Then there was a burst of laughter, and my father unlocked the door. There was no more talk about Virginia Hill.

I didn't hear of her again until twenty-five years later, when Annette Bening played her opposite Warren Beatty in the movie, *Bugsy*. There was no story about Senator Kefauver.

DAVY KEPT HIS PAST to himself, at least around me. He was not embarrassed by his history—not in the least—nor was he troubled that many of his friends and colleagues had been criminals, some of them notorious. Just the opposite: his whole life, Davy respected crooks more than judges. So there was no shame in his secrecy. It was more like modesty. My father was a truly unambitious man. He had, at least by the time I was old enough to recognize it, no interest in wealth or status. He had only a sporting interest in politics. His brother, my uncle Hye, was a supporter of the socialist CCF and had been some kind of communist in the 1930s, but Davy thought all governments corrupt, having, no doubt, done some of the corrupting himself. And yet he was a highly moral man, with a sense of propriety you would not expect in a man who made his living the way he did. He hardly drank, did not smoke (except cigars) and I never heard him tell a dirty joke. When I got old enough to ask him about sex, he sent me to my mother.

Gambling, however, was another story. Davy was not a gambler, not at all, but he made sure I knew all about it. In Davy's books, though it was

no sin, gambling was deeply foolish. 'The track is the one place the window cleans you,' he liked to say. Or he would repeat the advice Sky Masterson's father offered in *Guys and Dolls*, words I have known by heart for as long as I can remember: 'Son, someday, somewhere, a guy is going to come up to you and show you a nice brand-new deck of cards on which the seal is never broken, and this guy is going to offer to bet you that the jack of spades will jump out of this deck and squirt cider in your ear. But son, do not bet him, for as sure as you do, you are going to get an earful of cider.'

All the while I was growing up, my father conducted a personal, in-house, anti-gambling crusade. 'Don't never bet,' Davy liked to warn me, in an accent that would raise eyebrows today. He was quoting and imitating Sweet Lilies by the Wayside, the old man who once tended the water barrel in the backstretch at Dufferin Park. 'Don't never bet. How you think them hosses gets feeded?'

It is ironic that this is the fatherly advice I remember because, by all accounts, Davy knew more about betting on horses than anybody. And yet, he never bet when I knew him and rarely bet before that. The cops liked to call people in the gambling business 'gamblers', but for the most part, they were anything but. Abe Orpen would say, 'If you ask my advice, it is do not gamble; however, if you insist upon gambling, I'll take your action.' Mister Orpen, as he liked to be called, was, in his time—the last part of the nineteenth and the first part of the twentieth century—Ontario's most revered bookmaker. And he was the man who gave my father his start.

In 1916, when he was eleven, Davy peddled papers at the corner of King and York, just down the street from Orpen's King Street gambling club. Mister Orpen would buy his daily paper from Davy, and he noticed the ease with which the boy made change. Davy was born with a head for figures. Orpen started testing him, getting him to calculate payouts on bets laid at different odds. Davy answered instantly. And so Abe Orpen took him under his wing, and into the bookmaking business. Or so the family story goes.

Another version of Davy's induction into the gambling business goes like this: When he was a boy, Davy was crazy for horses. He loved their rippling muscle, their satin skin, and their intelligent eyes. So he would hang around the shed rows at Dufferin Park, 'Little Saratoga', the half-mile track Abe Orpen opened in downtown Toronto in 1903. The men in the

backstretch—there were no women allowed in those days—called my father 'Little Jockey', which is what he wanted to be, but he grew too big, too soon. Still there was never a shortage of work around the stables for an eager kid, and no shortage of lessons about horses for a boy with an observant eye and a keen mind. Davy took it all in, and everything he learned confirmed Sweet Lilies by the Wayside's counsel, offered gratis to any young hot walker or stable boy passing through his domain: 'How you gonna know what a critter gonna do dat sleeps standin' up?'

There is a third path that could have led Davy to the bookmaking business. In those years, it was common for bookies to use newsboys as their 'front ends'. A punter would place his bet with the newsboy, who would record it—in my father's case, in his head—and pass it on to the bookie, the 'back end', when he did his rounds. A newsboy with a head for figures was as good as gold to a bookie, and a job with a bookie was food on an otherwise lean table for an immigrant Jewish kid who slept on a row of boxes in the corner of the kitchen of a tenement in the Toronto slum called the Ward.

• • • 3. A gold coin • • •

DAVY WAS BORN aboard the SS *Sicilian* on January 15, 1905, three days
out of Liverpool in steerage. This was not supposed to happen. By the time
of the birth, my grandmother, Chava Bossin, was supposed to be reunited
with my grandfather. But the snares in an emigrant's path were many. There
were swindlers, corrupt border guards, officials enforcing arbitrary rules.
There were also Samaritans, individuals and organizations who sprang up
to help strangers like my grandmother make their way across Europe and
onto a ship headed for the *goldene medina*, the Promised Land of, in the
Bossins' case, Toronto. What delayed Chava is unknown. But she boarded
the *Sicilian* in the last days of her pregnancy, disguising the fact under a
greatcoat, hoping for the best.

My grandmother sailed from Liverpool with four children. She disem-
barked in Halifax with five. Davy would be the first Bossin to grow up
entirely in Canada and he would bear the brunt of his father's efforts to
replant his Old World Judaism in the dirt of a Toronto slum. The sporting
world that would offer Davy an escape from poverty and prejudice was
anathema to his father. Zussman beat Davy as a boy and fought with him
as a man. At the mere mention of my paternal grandfather, my mother's face
would darken. She had known him only at the end of his life, but could
not forgive him for what she felt he had done to Davy. My father's attitude
was more complex. For all their struggles, Davy held his father in the
respect my *zeyde* demanded.

My *zeyde*, my grandfather, Zussman Bossin, had arrived in Toronto in
1904, nine months before his wife and children. He was the first Bossin to
leave the Old Country for the new. Zussman had been born in 1866 in
Brusilov, a town near Kiev, in what was called the Pale of Settlement, the
area along the western edge of Russia to which Jews were restricted. He
was an Orthodox Jew, as most Jews were, and he was poor, as most Jews
were as well. He worked as a glazier and a carpenter, as his father had
before him. He was strong, stubborn, devout, and hard as nails.

Zussman served his six compulsory years in the military, starting in
the late 1880s. He was not pressed into decades of service as a child—the

Zussman Bossin (left), Motl Bossin and a friend. Immigrant men often posed for combined portraits to reduce the cost.

fate of some Jewish boys of twelve or even younger before the Russian conscription laws were liberalized in 1874.

As the stories have come down from grandparents and great-grandparents, the life of Jews in the nineteenth-century Russian military was hell. In reality, it was and it wasn't. The Czar's army was harsh and ill-provisioned for all, and undoubtedly it was worse for Jews, who, in addition to the common privations, were pressured to convert to Christianity. Jews were refused promotion and kept from plum posts. My grandfather, you will recall, was denied his victory in a drumming competition because he was a Jew.

But for all that, the ill-treatment the Jews received was not universal. Many officers did not share the anti-Semitism of the Russian Court, and they frequently did their best to undermine the most draconian anti-Jewish edicts coming from St Petersburg. Jewish soldiers and their Christian comrades often got along well, and some Jews made notable achievements while in uniform. One of my uncles liked to tell the story of a young Jewish cantonist (cadet) who was esteemed by his comrades for his extraordinary skill—at pilfering. His name was Khodulevich.[1] The boys in the cantonist battalions were particularly impoverished and underfed; they stole to survive. While officially forbidden, the theft of food was overlooked by officers and even surreptitiously admired. Khodulevich was the best thief in the battalion, as deft as a magician.

There came a day when Czar Alexander II himself attended the battalion's manoeuvres. The cantonists' commander, General Treshkin, bragged to Alexander that his boys could steal anything from anyone. Alexander assured his General that they could not steal anything from him. They bet on it. After the drills, General Treshkin introduced Cantonist Khodulevich to the Czar. Khodulevich presented Alexander with the watch from Alexander's pocket.

My grandfather finished his military service in 1890, at twenty-four. It was time for him to marry. His mother, Surah Leah, contacted the *shadkhn*, the matchmaker, who suggested a bride from a neighbouring town. The three of them were on their way to meet her family when they stopped at a market. There, Surah Leah spotted an acquaintance, the Widow Slapos-

1 This is a true story. According to Yohanan Petrovsky-Shtern's definitive study, *Jews in the Russian Army*, the incident occurred in 1856.

nick. With her was her daughter, Dvora. Dvora was a beautiful girl. Zussman was smitten. Or he may have thought, if his bride was to be chosen arbitrarily, why not someone beautiful? He suggested he marry Dvora instead. The match was re-arranged, and Zussman and Dvora wed.

I once asked one of my aunts if my grandfather and Dvora loved each other. 'Love was never involved in marriages in those days,' she said. I asked if, like Tevye and Golde in *Fiddler on the Roof*, they 'learned to love each other.' She said, 'I don't think so.'

THE BOSSIN HOME in Brusilov was on the outskirts of town. It had a dirt floor which the women whitewashed every week. The hearth served as both stove and furnace. Three Bossin families shared the house: Zussman and his family, Zussman's younger brother Motl and his; and Zussman and Motl's parents, Leib and Surah Leah. All told, there were six adults and eight children in the house. Each family slept in one room, three to a bed. As well, to help make ends meet, the Bossins took in a boarder.

The family spent the Sabbath together. Then the men left for the week to ply their trade as glaziers. They each headed for a different town with a cart carrying glass, wood and tools, looking for windows to mend. They would sleep in barns or wherever they could, cooking for themselves in order to keep kosher. They only returned home for the next Sabbath. Meanwhile, the women tended the children, the house, the goats and the cow. The boys went to *cheder*, Jewish religious school, at least when they were small; the girls did not. In the winter, the children stayed indoors because they did not have shoes. There were no toys and no prized possessions in the Bossin home. Still, there was enough food, even if it was, as one of my aunts recalled, 'herring and potatoes, herring and potatoes, herring and potatoes.'

So home life was close to the bone, but not impossible. Town life was much the same. Brusilov had a Christian majority and a Jewish minority. The Bossins were wary of the gentiles but they got along with their Christian neighbours, taking care to do so.

Conditions in the Old Country were never good for Jews, though the degree of hardship varied from decade to decade and place to place. Ironically, in the latter years of the nineteenth century, Jews in the Pale envied their German cousins for the tolerance and liberality Germany offered them. In the Russian empire, things were more precarious. Czar Alexander III, who inherited the crown when his father was assassinated in 1881, was

fiercely anti-Semitic. Year after year, new laws were proclaimed, restricting where Jews could live, where they could travel and what they could do. In 1881 and 1882, there was a wave of pogroms. In 1891, Jews were driven out of Moscow, Kiev and other cities.

DVORA AND ZUSSMAN had four children between 1892 and 1898. In between, she gave birth to twins who died. In approximately 1901, she again became pregnant with twins. She and the twins died in the birth. Zussman was left a widower with four children under ten. Surah Leah, Zussman's mother, urged him to remarry. 'You can't take care of all these children yourself,' she told him.

'If I get married again, I'll have even more children to feed,' he replied.

But Surah Leah already had a match in mind. Living across the street from the Bossins was a widow who was known to be barren. Chava Wisotsky was born in 1875. The Wisotskys were a wealthy family. Chava's father, Duvid, was a furrier. She had had two brothers, but they were robbed and murdered while taking a wagonload of furs to Kiev.

The Wisotskys arranged for Chava to marry an old man whom she had never seen. He, it turned out, had tuberculosis. On their wedding night, all night long, she said, he coughed and spat. She disliked him intensely and left him. He died not long after and, as Jewish law demanded, she was betrothed to his younger brother. But Chava refused to marry him, and when she was twenty-seven or twenty-eight, she moved into the house across the street from the Bossins. There she got to know Zussman's children. Surah Leah watched Chava playing with them. She knew Chava was a widow and childless—a perfect wife for Zussman. The wedding took place in 1904. Soon after, Zussman left for Canada.

THE SEEDS OF EMIGRATION had been germinating in the rocky soil of the Bossins' lives for years. The events of 1903 settled it. Pogroms had begun again, culminating in a massacre in Kishinev that shocked the world: in two days, fifty Jews were killed, five hundred were injured, girls and women were raped, and hundreds of homes were destroyed. The atrocity—encouraged by the authorities and shrugged off by the police—made international headlines. It horrified Russian Jews.

That same year, Brusilov had its own pogrom, though it was abortive. The story goes that the ringleader fell off his horse (or was pushed) and broke his leg. The perpetrators—young toughs from neighbouring towns

Leib and Surah Leah

who had converged on Brusilov—retired to tend to him and did not come back. But the experience was terrifying. My aunt Ethel remembered being packed, ready to flee, listening in strict silence to the crash of breaking glass in the town. Fortunately, the Bossin house was on the outskirts and the vandals never got that far.

For many Jews, the 1903 pogroms were the last straw. Talk of emigration was everywhere. Zussman, however, hesitated. He was nearly forty, he had a family to feed and they were, at least, fed. And emigration was a journey from which you did not return. Zussman's choice was to stay. But my great-grandmother, Surah Leah, once again had a different idea.

SURAH LEAH's grandchildren, my aunts and uncles, remembered her as a sweet old lady who looked like Whistler's Mother. She wore a dirndl skirt and apron, with a pocket full of sour raspberry candies for children whose

hands were well scrubbed. When grandchildren were born, Surah Leah would make them down pillows, plucking the goose, and separating the down from the feathers by hand into two galvanized metal tubs. She wore a bonnet over a shaven head, taking the *mikve* baths and upholding the other traditions of Orthodox Jewish womanhood. To all appearances, she deferred to my great-grandfather, Leib.

But it was Surah Leah who set the course the Bossins would take through the twentieth century. She persuaded Zussman to remarry and she persuaded him to emigrate. Chaya Gitl, Zussman's sister, influenced him as well. Chaya Gitl was clairvoyant. She read Zussman's cards and told him, 'Save your money, you are going on a long journey.' Whether the message came from the cosmos or from Surah Leah, Zussman heeded it and arranged passage to Toronto, where he had a distant cousin.

There he received the news that Chava was not barren after all. Her first marriage, it turned out, had never been consummated. Zussman saved what he could and borrowed the rest of the money he needed to send tickets for Chava and the children to sail to Canada. And so Davy came to be born on the SS *Sicilian*. Notified of the birth in steerage, the Captain visited Chava and gave her a gold coin. As was the maritime custom, Davy was offered free passage for life on the ships of the Allen Line. He never took the offer up. The gold coin was spent as soon as Chava reached shore, but the Bossins have been talking about it ever since.

THE SICILIAN docked at Halifax, where Chava and her children cleared immigration and boarded a train for Toronto. Zussman met them at Union Station, and took them home to a three-room flat in the Ward, officially St John's Ward. The Ward was as unsavoury a slum as Canada has ever seen. By 1905, when Chava arrived in the *goldene medina*, the Ward had been a slum for fifty years. Now it was a ghetto as well.

St John's Ward covered a square mile of Toronto's downtown, bounded by College Street on the north and Queen Street on the south, Yonge Street on the east and University Avenue on the west. The hub was Eaton's clothing factory. While Eaton's would not hire Jews in its department store, where they would be seen by the customers, Jews made up 80 percent of its clothing-manufacturing work force. Working conditions were deplorable, as they were throughout the *shmata* industry, leading to the Eaton's strike in 1912. The workers lost. Bad as conditions at the T. Eaton Company were, an Eaton's job was a job, and a better job than many

The Ward c. 1911

of the inhabitants of the Ward had, working as navvies, digging the sewer system for Toronto's wealthy neighbourhoods. It would be years before the sewers built by men from the Ward reached the Ward itself.

In 1911, when my father was six, Charles Hastings, the medical officer of health for the City of Toronto, investigated conditions in the Ward and reported, 'contaminated water, overcrowding, windowless rooms, unsanitary water closets, filthy lanes and back alleys, cesspools rising up through back lots. There are houses ... where waste and slop water are thrown into the yard, where the windows cannot be opened on summer days because of the smell.' The Hastings report shocked Toronto. The city fathers decried the conditions in which the immigrants lived (and the norms by which they lived as well). On the role of landlords, the lack of regulation, and the paucity of services, they were silent.

In their first years in Toronto, the Bossins found themselves poorer than they had been in the Pale of Settlement from which they had fled. There, at least they had a cow, goats, chickens and a garden. Still, in the Ward there were no pogroms, no anti-Jewish laws (at least none proclaimed officially), and the torments inflicted by the Cossacks were reduced to the occasional arbitrary demands of an Irish, English or Scottish cop. The streets of the Ward were not paved with gold, but they were paved.

Zussman and Chava operated a junk store. When he had first arrived in Toronto, my grandfather worked as a glazier, as he had in the old country. He carried his tools and glass in a wooden box on his back. He also

Zussman and Chava

worked as a paper-hanger and a carpenter, but then a nail he was hammering broke and flew into his eye. He lost the sight of the eye and, with it, his profession. After that, he became a dealer of second-hand tools and other used goods. He would head out each day with a horse and cart, finding or buying anything broken-down or worn out. Zussman was a *latootnik*, a fixer. He could fix anything that was repairable. He did this, he claimed, by making himself small, slipping into the mechanism and looking around for the problem. Chava minded the store and the children. Somehow the business supported them, even with my grandfather contributing generously to the *russische shul*, the Russian immigrants' synagogue. This he did, much to the chagrin of my grandmother who was charged with the task of feeding them all on what was left. Davy was the first of seven children borne by my formerly barren grandmother. In the end she raised eleven children. 'Zi kindlt oyfeles vi ketzlech,' my grandfather complained in mock, and perhaps real, exasperation. 'She puts them out like kittens.'

Poverty marked all the Bossins, though it marked each of them differently. My aunt Celia blamed it for the unfulfilled promise in her life. My uncle Art credited it for his successes. It was harder on the girls than the four Bossin boys, who spoke of their childhood fondly. As children they saw little anti-Semitism, except for scuffles with other racially homogeneous gangs of kids. Almost everyone they knew was a Jew.

Whatever the deprivations of the Ward, it offered Davy and his siblings something their parents never had—freedom. Back in the Pale, children were rarely out of their parents' sight. As soon as they were old enough to help, much of their day was spent on chores. But in the teeming streets of the Ward, Davy and his brothers experienced something entirely new: anonymity. A boy could get into all sorts of mischief.

Zussman fought hard to hold back the Canadian tide. He beat his sons, as he had been beaten by his father, Leib. He hit his daughters. 'Pa wore a workman's leather belt,' my uncle Art told me, 'and he could whip that thing off and strike like a cobra.' He said it with a smile I never understood. Davy bore the brunt of Zussman's doomed effort to reconstruct the traditions of the *shtetl*. If religion could have been beaten into a boy, his oldest Canadian son would have been a rabbi. Davy, however, found his vocation on the street.

If, as it proudly proclaimed, Toronto had a church on every corner, in the Ward it had a crap game in every alley. And every crap game needed a boy to stand watch and whistle if he saw a cop. A three-card-monte game

needed a strong-armed kid to be the Table. The Table would stand with an open newspaper across his outstretched arms. The newspaper was the surface on which the money was put down and the cards dealt. If a cop came, the Table folded the newspaper, catching the money and cards inside, and innocently hurried off with a newspaper under his arm.

In the Ward, there were crap games for pennies and for dollars; there were bootleggers and bookies who could always 'use a good boy', and there were street gangs to join or fight. Boxing was a popular pastime which all the Bossin boys learned and, from time to time, employed. And there was the new world sport, baseball. The Judeans were city champions. True, they had a pair of ringers: they had a left-handed pitcher who came in from wherever his people lived, miles to the west. The Judeans paid him two dollars a game and streetcar fare. They also had a *goyische* first baseman. 'Where were we gonna find a tall Jew?' one of my uncles explained.

Davy and his brothers loved baseball. My father was one of the bat boys for the Toronto Maple Leafs when World War I began. My grandfather could fathom neither the sport nor his sons' attraction to it. '*Far vos zol a yingl alt genug arbeiten, geh aus onshtot shpiln mit a ball!*' Zussman exclaimed. Why should a boy, who is old enough to work, be out playing ball?

'Pop, this is America,' Davy explained. 'Babe Ruth earns $50,000 a year!'

Zussman shook his head. '*Fur makhn yenem?*' For doing that?

THOUGH THE BOSSIN BOYS found time to play, they also worked, peddling newspapers as soon as they were old enough to protect the proceeds from bigger boys. Davy sold papers at one of the corners at King and York, his brother Hye at another, and his youngest brother, Art, at a third. The proprietorship of a corner was dependent upon the newsboy's ability to fight for it. Fortunately, Hye was a newsboy boxing champ. Art was another. Art liked to boast that he once won a prize for boxing and a prize for oratory in the same week. Hye and Art both went from newsboy to printer's devil. Davy, however, had impressed one of Toronto's most prominent and colourful citizens, the city's premier impresario of gambling, legal and illegal.

• • • 4. Mister Orpen • • •

IF THE FAMILY STORY is true, when Davy was eleven years old, Abe
Orpen saw a spark in him and took him into the business of horse-race
gambling. From the surviving accounts of Mister Orpen, it is certainly
possible. Abram Orpen was both generous and shrewd, a soft touch and a
deft judge of character, who liked to say, 'Men and horses run to form.' He
cut a unique figure in Toronto's history. 'He played for the game and not
the chips,' a reporter wrote when Orpen died in 1937 at eighty-three. He
was big (three hundred pounds, by some accounts), without an ounce of
hypocrisy in him. He became one of Toronto's richest men, but preferred
the fraternity of the backstretch to the collegiality of the York Club. Mis-
ter Orpen, as he liked to be called, was a true *mensch*, a seat-of-the-pants
humanitarian who, in the words of the *Toronto Telegram*, 'loved humanity
more than many a prelate.' If he really was Davy's mentor, Davy was a
lucky man.

In *Down the Stretch, Recollections of a Pioneer Sportsman and Journalist*,
William A. Hewitt, father of the hockey commentator Foster Hewitt,
recalled his first encounter with Mr Orpen. At the time, the early 1890s,
Hewitt was a cub reporter for the *Toronto News*. One day, he was walking

along King Street when, to his surprise, Mr Orpen hailed him. They had never met, but no one in Toronto, at least among the sporting set, would fail to recognize the dean of the city's bookmakers.

'Mr Hewitt,' Orpen said, 'my agents tell me that you've been placing a lot of bets on a lot of races, and that you have not been doing very well. They say you are betting too often and too much. What salary do you draw?'

Hewitt made nine dollars a week.

'William,' Orpen told him, 'you cannot win, not in the long run. And you cannot win at all if you need the money. A wealthy man can hold on until he hits a winner or two. But you cannot do that on nine dollars a week.' Then Orpen offered Hewitt a proposition. 'Come to my office any day for the next month and you can place a bet on any horse, running at any track in America. One bet a day. I will give you 2-to-1 odds every time. Don't leave any money. At the end of the month we will tally up.'

At the end of the month, Hewitt owed Orpen eighteen dollars, half his month's salary. Orpen invited him into his private office, an alcove separated from the main floor of the gambling club by a thick velvet curtain. 'William, I hope you have learned something,' Orpen said. He offered to forgive the debt. Hewitt insisted on paying it. 'It was a cheap lesson that saved me thousands,' he would write.

Abe Orpen taught many that lesson, including, it would seem, my father, who insistently passed it on to me. For Orpen, gambling was one of life's delights if kept in its place—a dessert, not a meal. It was convivial, stimulating, educational. 'Over the poker table,' he said, 'a young man can learn his follies and the ways to control them more cheaply and more quickly than any other way.'

ABRAM MICHAEL ORPEN was born in Toronto in 1854 to an Irish Protestant family. His father, a railway paymaster, died in a train wreck when Abe was still a boy. His mother apprenticed him to a carpenter, dismissing his protests by saying, 'It was good enough for Our Lord, and it is good enough for you.'

Orpen credited his apprenticeship with setting him on the road his life would take, but not in the way his mother intended. In the last days of his indenture, he was working on the new Toronto Customs House. One morning, he was walking a beam fifty feet in the air, carrying one end of a long plank. His mate, at the other end, slipped and fell into the building,

catching himself on a joist. Orpen was thrown outward and would have fallen to his death but for a flat of bricks that was being hauled up. He landed on it as lightly as Errol Flynn and escaped the incident unscathed.

The next day, Orpen went to his boss and asked him to sign his journeyman's papers. The boss did. Orpen took his coat from the rack and said, 'Do you see what I'm doing?'

'Sure,' the boss said, 'you are putting on your coat.'

'That is just what I am doing,' Orpen said, 'and I am never again going to take my coat off to do a day's work as long as I live.'

He never did. With his coat and vest characteristically buttoned, he started a brick works and a lumber business; he exported liquor and imported watermelons (with the occasional crate of bourbon underneath). He bought the Alhambra Hotel on Church Street, a favorite saloon of the sporting crowd. As publican, he offered to flip a coin, double or nothing, for the cost of a drink. It cost him nothing—at the end of the day, his receipts were the same—but his customers loved it. (Later in his life, when he was negotiating the sale of an office building to Sir Isaac Killam, the publisher of the *Toronto Mail and Empire*, Orpen offered to settle the matter by the same method. 'Isaac,' he suggested, 'why don't we just toss a penny and see whether you raise your price $20,000 or I drop mine $20,000?' Killam refused.)

At the Alhambra, Orpen observed the workings of probability in the games played at his tables. He was intrigued in particular by the bookmakers, and their rich knowledge of horses and men.

A BOOKMAKER is not a gambler. One who is won't last long. A bookie is really a broker. He earns his daily bread on the 'vigorish', the 10 percent difference between what the loser has bet and what the bookie pays out to the winner. Which horse wins and which loses is incidental. A smart bookie is not trying to beat his customers. Rather, he sets his odds so as to spread the bets as evenly as possible over all the horses in a race. He offers a temptingly high payout on a long shot; he discourages bets on the favourite by promising only a minimal return if the horse wins. The fact that so many customers make poor choices, based on hunches, superstition or erroneous tips, is just icing; the bookie's cake is the vigorish.

In these days of state-sanctioned off-track betting, most bookies no longer handle bets on horseracing. Team sports have replaced the track as the bookmakers' mainstay. And even where a bookie will still accept a bet

on a horse, he no longer determines the payout himself. Now it is based on the exact amount bet on each horse through the pari-mutuel machines at the track. Under the pari-mutuel system—by law, the betting system used at all tracks in North America—a horse may begin the day as a long shot, but then experience a wave of support at the betting windows, and end up paying only a modest return. (The total proceeds from the losing bettors have to be divided among the increased number of winning bettors; therefore each winner gets a smaller share of the pool.) And that payout is further reduced by the track's and the government's own vigorish, a rake-off that can run 17 percent or more. So, before the horses leave the gate, the punter's dollar has dropped to 83 cents. What the track pays out, the bookie pays out. With a 17 percent handicap, only the most knowledgeable, cautious and disciplined bettor can come out ahead in the long run. The racetrack adage, 'All horse players die broke,' has a solid mathematical basis.

In the years before World War I, when the pari-mutuel system came in, Abe Orpen quit bookmaking. He mourned the loss of the profession's creativity to the new machines. Setting the right odds was, for Orpen, a source of pride. Now, he complained, the machines and the high rake-off meant that the only people who would make money at the tracks would be the men who owned them. So, starting in 1903, Orpen bought or built racetracks. By the early 1930s he owned six of them.

Orpen was as exceptional a track owner as he was as a bookie. His little half-mile track in downtown Toronto, Dufferin Park—where Sweet Lilies by the Wayside taught Davy 'how them hosses gets feeded'—was a model of democracy and classlessness, front and backstretch. In the grandstand there were no separate jockey-club seats or owner's boxes. Dufferin's shed rows were, for those who worked and slept in them, the most accommodating of any track in America. At Orpen's tracks, blacks worked alongside whites; at most others, they were restricted to the most menial positions.

Orpen also proved an innovative and canny race promoter. In 1920, after he had opened Kenilworth Park in Windsor, Ontario, he put up an $80,000 purse—an unheard-of amount at the time—for a match race between the legendary Man o' War and Sir Barton, the first winner of racing's Triple Crown. The press called it 'The Race of the Century', but as a contest, it was a dud. Man o' War won easily. Still it remains one of the most viewed horse races of all time. It was the first race ever filmed, another

Orpen innovation. He had cameras placed at intervals all around the track, and then had the footage edited together. The race can still be watched on YouTube, nearly a century after the fact.

PLAYING THE HORSES became an ever more popular pastime over the course of Abe Orpen's (and Davy's) lifetime, even as public approval of gambling waxed and waned. When Orpen first took up bookmaking the trade was legal, at least for bookies operating at the track. Orpen liked to say that what he did was 'not quite legal and not quite illegal.' But a generation or two of North American reformers convinced the public that, like drinking liquor, gambling was a sin and a menace; or at least they convinced enough voters to elect those who professed to think so. In fact, Canadians continued to gamble even as the reformers they elected enacted laws to stop them.

As with Prohibition, the laws against gambling sprang from a mix of idealism, hypocrisy and elitism. The brew was the spirit of the times, its manifestations everywhere. Toronto, for instance, had a forty-man committee—it included no women—known as the 'theatre purifiers'. At the purifiers' recommendation, theatres, plays and their casts could be, and were, prosecuted for indecency.

Underlying this zeal for moral uplift was an almost feudal acceptance of social class. From the get-go, the Criminal Code of Canada allowed betting at the track; if you had the leisure to attend the races, you could, prior to the advent of the pari-mutuel machines, place your bets with one of Mister Orpen's associates—with the full acquiescence of the state. But when a worker, who could not spend the day at the races, bet the same horse with his bookie back in town (often another Orpen associate), he committed a crime. This was a contradiction the reformers could never explain away.

The campaign against bookmaking was also fuelled by racism. The public's taste for gambling grew concurrently with the Great Migration, and the gambling business was one of the few professions open to Jews and other 'foreigners'. So the business took on a Jewish (or Italian, or Chinese) cast. True to the racial attitudes of the time, the foreigners' success in the field was attributed not to their acumen but to dishonesty, and the foreigners' presence was deemed a threat to the sport—as if chicanery was unknown in racing before the advent of Jewish bookies. 'Much of the trouble,' wrote Canadian racing historian E. King Dodds in 1909 'is directly traceable to the fact that a low class of Jew gamblers have, during the past

few years, invaded the ring.' Dodds' prejudice was shared by many an Anglo-Saxon politician, ranking police officer, judge and leading citizen. Henry Ford, the automobile magnate, for example, wrote in his pamphlet, *The International Jew*, 'The bane of American sports today is the presence of a certain type of Jew, not as participant, but as an exploiter and corrupter.' In reality bookmakers rarely, if ever, fixed a race. Bookies rely on the predictability of events, the balance between bettors. A fixed race throws their best calculations out the window and can cost them dearly. However, the fact that the accusations against the 'foreign' bookies were unfounded made them no less prevalent. The prejudice would still be there in the 1940s, fuelling the Crown's dogged pursuit of my father.

Mister Orpen, however, believed no such guff, neither the racial slurs (he went out of his way to employ Jews and other minorities) nor the pontifications on the evils of gambling and the laws they spawned. 'You cannot legislate away a man's idea of pleasure,' he said.

That wisdom was not, however, shared by the authorities (nor is it to this day) and so Orpen spent much of his life as a quasi-outlaw, though a highly moral, well respected, frequently beloved one. By and large, the law let him be. If he was not exactly Family Compact, he was cut from the same cloth, and certainly he was no foreigner. For his part, Orpen made frequent and generous political and charitable contributions and thereby exercised considerable influence. It was said that a policeman could not be promoted in Toronto without Abe Orpen's blessing. He further protected himself by discreetly closing down his gambling operations—for a time—when tipped off that a crackdown was imminent. Once when Orpen was called to testify before the Toronto Police Commission, he was asked if he ever received a warning in advance of a raid on his club. 'Oh yes,' he told the Commission, 'I always know when the police are coming.' This caused a great stir, and he was asked how he knew. 'They ring the doorbell,' he explained. 'No one else does.'

Some of Orpen's charitable works were self-serving, but much of his largesse was simply generous, a contribution sorely needed in a country without a social safety net. At the height of the Great Depression, Orpen organized and funded a soup kitchen in Toronto's armouries. For two years it served two meals a day to five hundred people. On Orpen's eightieth birthday, in 1934, the Mayor of Toronto, the Premier of Ontario, and the Prime Minister of Canada all sent letters of congratulation. 'I will start to think I am a respectable citizen if this keeps up,' Orpen told a reporter.

Acknowledgement by Canada's leaders came late, but down on the street, Mr Orpen had long been admired and loved by those, like Davy, to whom he offered a helping hand. It was widely known that, every Friday morning, the door to Orpen's office was open to anyone who wanted to see him. Sometimes the line stretched around the block. Sammy Luftspring, the champion welterweight boxer who fought with the Star of David on his trunks, joined the line one day in 1935, when he did not have the money to travel to the Canadian Boxing Championships in Edmonton. He recalled the day in his autobiography, *Call Me Sammy*.

'No matter how good you were,' he wrote, 'and let us not mince words, I was good—if you didn't have the dough, you didn't go. So one morning, I walked down to Mr Orpen's club on King Street. When I got there, I discovered that half of Toronto was there ahead of me.'

Luftspring joined the line and eventually squeezed onto a bench outside Orpen's office to await his audience. A man came out, and one of Luftspring's bench mates gave him a nudge. 'See, that guy got something,' he pointed out. 'You see how he's got his hand in his pocket? If a guy comes out with his hand in his pocket, it's because he's got some money in it, and he's scared to death to let go of it.'

By the time Luftspring's turn came, he was not hopeful. 'I wanted money to go to Edmonton, but there were mothers there with sick kids and no heat, and so on and so forth. But I went in, and there was Mr Orpen sitting back behind his desk, with his coat and vest all buttoned up like a church deacon. "What is it, Sammy?" he said.' Orpen, a regular at boxing events, had seen many of Luftspring's fights.

Luftspring told Orpen that, without help, he could not go to the Canadian championships.

'And if you go, Sammy, do you think you'll win?' Orpen asked him.

'Mister Orpen,' he said, 'I've won seventy fights. I can lick any man in the country my weight.'

'Well, Sammy,' Orpen replied, 'I think you can too. How much will it cost you?'

Luftspring just stood there. He had no idea.

Orpen opened the cash box he kept on his desk and took out two fifty-dollar bills. Luftspring had never seen a fifty-dollar bill.

'Here,' Orpen said, 'this ought to do it.'

'I've taken some pretty good hits and rolled with them,' Luftspring recalled, 'but this time, my eyes filled up. I couldn't say anything. I don't

Sammy Luftspring

know if I even thanked him. All I remember is, there was no way I could keep my hand out of my pocket. I held on to those two fifties so tight, I practically had the ink squeezed out by the time I got back to Kensington.'

IF I COULD SUBMIT a list of questions to my father's ghost, the first would be whether the story about him selling newspapers to Mister Orpen in 1916 was true. I want it to be true—it is so cinematic—but I know I come from a family of story-tellers who, like A.J. Liebling's Honest Rainmaker, 'diverge from recorded history only to improve upon it.' Still, I lean towards believing the family account, for most everything I have learned about Orpen's outlook I saw in my father. And, since I see in myself more and more of Davy every year, I have to wonder just what I may have inherited from this prominent but unsung lion of Toronto's past. If 'men and horses run to form,' as Orpen believed, how much of my form traces back to Mister Orpen?

Davy, of course, never talked about such things, and his connection with Orpen fell under the cloak of his silence. He did, however, tell one story about him, and the twinkle in his eye reflected his admiration. The account seemed far-fetched at the time, but the Toronto newspapers of the day bear it out in every unlikely detail. The more I know about Orpen (and about Davy), the less surprising that seems.

When he was eighty-two, Abram Orpen was kidnapped. 'Kidnapping' is what the newspapers called it. In fact, it was not much of a kidnapping; it was more of a robbery, and it was a poor job of that.

By 1937, Orpen's sons managed his operations including the National Sporting Club, the family's big gambling hall at the mouth of the Humber River, just west of Toronto's city limits. Mister Orpen only went out to the club occasionally, and when he did it was mainly to oversee the gardens.

The National Sporting Club operated six days a week. Sundays, like everything else in Ontario, it was closed; flouting the gambling laws was one thing, disobeying the Lord's Day Act was another. So the three armed men who set out to rob the National Sporting Club chose a Sunday night to break in. One of them was, ostensibly, a safe-cracker, but after a few hours of effort at the club's safe, he gave up. The robbers hastily revised their plan and decided to await the arrival next morning of the manager with the combination. But, as fate would have it, the manager had business in the city that Monday morning, and did not come. Mister Orpen, however, chose that day to go out to the club and inspect the gardens.

When he arrived, he was met at gunpoint. The robbers demanded the combination. Orpen told them that he had no idea what the combination was; he had nothing to do with that end of the business anymore. 'But,' he said, 'if you put those weapons away, and tell me what it is you need like civilized men, perhaps I can be of assistance.' The robbers demanded five thousand dollars, and ordered Orpen to return with them to his home to get the money. Orpen told them absolutely not, it would frighten his wife to death, and anyway, he did not keep that kind of money at home. 'However,' he said, 'I have a counter-proposal. We can drive to my bank, and when it opens, I will withdraw six hundred dollars and give it to you, no questions asked.'

'Sure, and as soon as you get in the bank, you'll peach us out,' one of them said.

'I will do no such thing,' Orpen told them. 'I am a man of my word. You can ask anyone.'

The thieves conferred and then agreed in principle, but still demanded $5000. Mister Orpen said he would come up to a thousand, but he would not go a penny higher. They could do what they wanted with him, but they would not get anything out of it, except a lot of trouble.

The men accepted his offer. They drove back into the city to the bank. There Orpen withdrew $1000, returned to the car and gave it to his captors, just as he had said. They all shook hands. Orpen told them they ought to find another line of work. Then he invited them to come back to the club. 'Come as my guests,' he said. 'It will give me a chance to win my money back.'

When the story broke, it made front-page headlines for days. The police investigated, but never caught the robbers. The search was hampered because, true to his word, Mister Orpen refused to identify his assailants.

• • • 5. Sack's two dollars • • •

THIS IS THE EARLIEST picture I have of my father. It was taken by a street photographer outside Zussman's store. There are no pictures of Davy as a boy or an adolescent. Photographs were a luxury the Bossins could not afford.

Stories from Davy's youth are almost as scarce as pictures. There is the Orpen story, and the argument with Zussman about Babe Ruth. There is the time Davy's teacher kept him after school and he locked her in the cloakroom and ran off. He cannot have been more than eleven, because he was out of school by twelve. (The legal age for leaving school was sixteen, but it was not enforced during World War I. In the Ward, it was loosely enforced at the best of times.) The cloakroom caper was, unfortunately for Davy, soon reported to his father, providing another occasion for Zussman's belt to strike like a cobra.

Only one other story of Davy's childhood has survived. One day Zussman sent Hye, Davy's younger brother, to fetch him home. Hye caught up to Davy on a street corner but Davy refused to go back with him, and headed off with his gang. Hye followed after them, saying, 'Pa says, I gotta bring you back!' So Davy took the handful of coins from his pocket—from selling papers or who knows what—and threw them down on the sidewalk. In a family where every penny counted, Hye had to stop to gather the coins. By then Davy was gone.

He is not heard from again, at least by me, until his teens. Seventy-five years after the fact, one of his pals still remembered Davy leaning on the rail at Dufferin Park with the race card protruding from his pocket, offering tips for 10 percent of the winnings. Which is to say, by then, Davy was a tout.

Touting is the one racetrack profession that does not require capital, a boss, or a horse. Anyone can offer a tip, and many, if not most, punters are in the market. The demand is perennial, and the tout can service it at no risk: if his recommendation loses, it costs him nothing. Some touts are fly-by-night operators with a simple *modus operandi*. If there are six horses in contention, a resourceful and fast-moving tout might offer tips on all six, each at a different location in the grandstand. Then, after the race, he returns to the place where he predicted the winner. His customer is sure to pay up, because he will want more tips from such a reliable source.

Not all touts are con men, however. Some are knowledgeable and sincere; if they had a stake they would bet it. And a few touts—a very few— are true handicappers. Based on his subsequent success, I believe Davy was, even as a teenager, handicapping.

'Handicapping is not rocket science,' says the author and horsewoman Jane Smiley, 'it is harder'. No one can consistently predict the outcome of a horse race. There are too many variables. However, that same complexity offers a hard-working handicapper a rich field of information on which to base his choices. The form and history of race horses are logged with the obsessive thoroughness of baseball statistics or stock market performance charts.[1] A good handicapper will know the complete record of each horse. He will know how successful its parents, siblings and ancestors were. He will know what length of race the horse prefers; how it is affected by the weight it carries; how its works (practice runs) have been going; what weather, track surface and track conditions suit it; how it reacts to starting from different positions in the gate; and how the horse appears to be

1 While Abe Orpen believed that 'men and horses run to form', J.V. McAree, the great—and first—Canadian newspaper columnist, disagreed. 'Cheap horses,' he wrote, 'which is to say ninety per cent of all horses running, have no form. They keep on beating each other and losing to each other, just as different dice faces turn up. What they do today has little reference to what they will do next week, or what they did last. *Racing Form* is just about as useful, we suppose, as a dream book.'

feeling today, physically and mentally, as seen in the pre-race parade. The handicapper then needs to know the jockey and the trainer. Is this the kind of race a particular trainer is likely to try to win, or might he 'give the horse an easy one?' Is the jockey well matched to the horse and the conditions of the particular race? Finally the odds—which under the pari-mutuel system are not stable—must be taken into account, and, nowadays, the different betting alternatives (win, place, show, daily double, triactor, pick six and so on) weighed. No wonder that, whenever racing columnists' picks have been tracked over time, they wind up in the red.

Still, certain men are recognized for their extraordinary handicapping abilities, and Davy was one. When he died, the *Toronto Star* called him a 'noted handicapper', no faint praise. 'The highlight of Bossin's career,' the *Star* reported, 'came when, one day, he managed to pick all the winners, win, place and show, in all races.'

A lot of people told that story about my father. But there is a problem with it.

To do that, Davy had to correctly predict first-, second- and third-place winning horses in all 8 races, 24 money winners out of 24. The trouble is, the odds against doing so are astronomical. It is what statisticians call 'conditional probability'. The odds on the first winning choice must be multiplied by the odds on the second choice, and that total multiplied by the odds for the third choice, and so on, through 24 multiplications. The chances of having a perfect day are in the neighbourhood of one in 100 billion. By comparison, winning the 6/49 jackpot is a piece of cake. Being hit by lightning is downright imminent.

So I took the story with a grain of salt.

But. We used to have, when I was growing up, one of those dining room tables with a hinged table top. If you slid the top over, without unfolding it, a little hidden drawer was revealed. One day long after my father died, I looked in there and found, along with the dust, pencil stubs and dried-out elastics, two clipped-together issues of *The Canadian Racing and Financial News*, the scratch sheet my father once published. The first issue had, among the listings of the horses, the jockeys and the scratches, Davy's predictions for the day's races at Woodbine. Each one was circled in red pencil. The second issue, from the next day, had the results. They matched up perfectly. He had really done it—24 for 24. One shot in a hundred billion.

And yet he never bet. With, he knew, good reason. For if the chance

of doing that once is one in 100 billion, what was the likelihood of doing it again?

DESPITE THE OLD ADAGE, all horse players do not die broke. That is because, eventually, most of them give it up. They know when they are licked. The few who can afford a lifelong affair with the track are, perforce, disciplined men. Sack Sniderman, my father's old pal, was one of those. Davy had known him since their childhood in the Ward, before Sack was called Sack. Sniderman, named Nathan by his parents, was originally nicknamed Sad Sack, shortened from the expression 'sad sack of shit', the same phrase that would be bowdlerized and used for the name of the World War II comic strip. In Sack Sniderman's case, the nickname suited his boyhood physiognomy and expression. In both he resembled Eeyore, the woeful donkey in *Winnie the Pooh*. But as he matured, Sack's lachrymose look mellowed into the appearance of studiousness, which mirrored his nature. Sack was a thoughtful, patient and contented man, which made him an exception among horse players.

By trade, Sack had been a milkman for Borden's Dairy and his career, and his love of horses, dated back to the days when he would deliver milk in a horse-drawn wagon. Those were also the days when Mr Orpen would throw open the gates of Dufferin Park for the last two races. Sack would arrive with his milkman's change dispenser still attached to his belt. Being the sober young man he was, it did not cost him many quarters before he developed a conservative and methodical approach to betting. 'All my life,' he would say, 'I've heard about fellows who got rich playing the horses, but the funny thing is, I've never met any of them.'

Sack and Davy were peas in a pod, at least when it came to racetrack philosophy, and Davy loved to tell the story of one particular day in his friend's long career at the track:

'Behind that poker face, Sack was crazy about racing. He loved all the good things about the sport, the horses, the turf, the silks, the smells, the way the figures in the *Racing Form* came to life and thundered down the stretch.

'So when he retired from Borden's, any day there was a meeting, he would head for Dufferin Park, or take the streetcar to wherever they were racing. Sack could get away with that, because he was the most disciplined, systematic horse player you ever met. His system was as simple as can be. He would leave home with two dollars in his pocket, and he would hold onto them until he found a horse he considered a good bet. Then he bet the

Davy at Santa Anita

two dollars. If he lost, he considered it a cheap ticket to a day in heaven. If he won, he would bet it all on the next horse he figured for a winner. If he won again, he would do it again.'

Eventually, according to Davy, one unforgettable day at Long Branch (another Toronto-area track started by Abe Orpen), Sack saw that a colt he had been keeping an eye on was entered in the first race at very long odds. He bet his two dollars. The horse came in, and paid $28. As it happened, Sack also liked a horse running in the second race, so he bet the $28, and he won again. The horse paid $5. Sack now had $70.[2] He did not like any of the horses in the third race, or the fourth and did not bet, but he liked another long shot in the fifth. He bet the roll. Again his horse won; it paid $18. Sack now had $630. It was not Sack's custom to bet so frequently, but this was turning out to be an unusual day. He bet the whole stake on the sixth race and he won again, and he won again on the seventh. By then, Sack had over $16,000.

'At that point, most people would pack it in, or put the bulk of the money aside. But not Sack. He was as methodical as a clock. There was one more race, and it included a filly named Heaven Scent, who, in fact, went on to a profitable career. Sack took his entire stake and bet it on her.'

But Heaven Scent ran up the alley, as the expression goes. That day, she lost. According to Davy, when Sack got home his wife, Sadie, asked him, 'How did you do?'

'Same as always,' Sack Sniderman told her. 'I lost two dollars.'

2 The figure paid out is for a $2 bet. A winner listed as paying $5 pays back $2.50 for every dollar wagered.

• • • 6. The layoff man • • •

MANY A RACETRACK STORY revolves around a fixed race, and my father's anecdotes were no exception. Or perhaps it is just that those were the tales that stuck in my memory, because their underdog-beats-the-system motif appealed to a small, not-very-athletic boy. How many races were (or still are) fixed cannot be known. The number is greater than the industry will ever acknowledge and fewer than the folklore would suggest. At different times in different locales—the post-World-War-II years in southwestern Ontario, for instance—the meets were so suspect that the bookies would not accept bets on them. On the other hand, many have been the wagers placed on the basis of a rumour that a particular race was in the bag. As one track owner wisely observed, 'If people didn't believe the fourth race was fixed, I'd be out of business.'

The golden years of racetrack chicanery in Ontario ended with the 'Lady in Black' scandal, named for the woman who placed a last-minute bet of $2,100 on a long shot named North Drive, at Fort Erie in the summer of 1951. A suspicious clerk at the pari-mutuel window noticed an unusual customer placing an exorbitant bet on an unlikely horse, and he marked down the numbers of the tickets he issued. When the no-account North Drive turned out to win the race (paying $17) an investigation began. Two days later, the suspicious tickets were cashed in and the authorities pounced. The trail led to Swabby Swartz, a shady racetrack character well known to my father and others on the Ontario sporting scene. Swartz, it seems, had bribed all eight jockeys. He paid seven of them 200 dollars each to pull their mounts, and promised the eighth, North Drive's rider, a $200 bonus if he won. Further investigation revealed that Swartz and his cohorts had fixed, or attempted to fix, at least seven other races at Fort Erie that summer and had won over $100,000 in the process. They accomplished this even though in one case, the horse, whose victory Swartz had orchestrated, stumbled and limped home last. In another race, a no-chance nag, whose jockey Swabby had not bothered to bribe, streaked past the sure thing, winning the race and paying 37 to 1. For his part in the North Drive swindle, Swartz was sentenced to three months in jail.

My favourite of my father's stories of racetrack chicanery was about Morris Fishman, and I heard it, like so many other of his recollections, on a muggy summer night at Maple Leaf Stadium. Davy and his cronies always gathered in the cheap seats in the upper reaches of the stands. An aisle separated us from the more expensive boxes closer to the field. On this night, someone pointed to a small, wiry man walking along that aisle. He had curly grey hair and the weathered skin of someone who spent most of his time outdoors. His hands were large and muscular; they looked like Michelangelo's David's. He turned into the box seats below us.

'Hey, isn't that Morris Fishman?'

'Who is Morris Fishman?' The man who asked was not a regular in my father's crowd, and he was not a Torontonian, nor a follower of horse racing. If he were, he would have known that Morris Fishman was one of the most esteemed trainers (and sometime horse owner) in the country.

Morris Fishman became the topic of the night. Stories flew back and forth about him and his horses: about how, when Fishman was flat broke, he borrowed a thousand dollars to buy High Honors and turned him into one of the best handicap racers the country ever saw. They talked about Canada's Teddy, Mugwump, North York and Be Brief, champions all; about the time, back in his jockey days, when Fishman rode four winners in six races on the card at Bowie, and would have won the other two races as well, if he hadn't been ordered to pull the horses. What brand of whiskey

Morris drank for breakfast was debated. Naturally, Fishman's lifetime suspension for race fixing was a hot topic. The ruling was still contentious thirty years after the fact.

'Anti-Semite bastards! They sure stuck it up his ass! What was he, seventeen years old? He was just a kid. And they wouldn't lift the ban for seven years, for chrissake. Seven years! By then he was too big to ride. And he never even fixed the race!'

'We'll all be *alte kakers* in the old folks' home, and you'll still be bitching about it. Morris never beefed about it as much as you.'

'I'll tell you one thing, if I ever wanted a jockey to pull a horse, Morris would be the guy. Did you see those hands? I remember the time he was in that hotel fire in Atlanta. He was stuck on the sixth floor. It was terrible, over a hundred people were killed. The bastards who owned the place didn't have any alarms or fire escapes or nothing. It was a miracle Morris got out. He tied bed sheets and blankets together and lowered himself down. He was a tough son of a bitch.'

'They say he had the strongest hands in Canadian racing. He could stop an elephant going for a bale of hay.'

'I wouldn't have thought slowing a horse down was a great virtue in a jockey.' This was the visitor again.

'It is a virtue, all right, if the jockey wants to work regular.'

'Hey, Davy, you knew Fishman. Did those kids fix the race?'

Davy, who had not joined the conversation, put down his paper. 'Never happened,' he said. 'But Morris never complained. He said they just hadn't done it yet.

'That stuff went on all the time in those days, before they had all the cameras. The trainer would say, "Give him an easy one." Morris told me one day he got a call from one outfit. When he got to the barn, the trainer showed him a big chestnut stallion, fit as a fiddle, ears pricked, head high. The horse looked like he could go neck and neck with Whirlaway. But the trainer says, "Morris, give him an easy one today. I want you to break late, and keep him in the back. Then move up to fifth or sixth place, and just hold him there. But keep your eye on his stride, and tell me after, how he woulda done if you let him run." Morris did just that. He brought the horse in fifth.

'When he got back to the barn, the trainer says to him, "Well, could he win it?"

'"Oh yeah," Morris says. "I give him a couple cracks with the whip and he'd fly past those four."

"'Good,' the trainer says. "We run him next week against the same bunch. He should go up at a pretty good price. You wanna make some money, bet him up."

"'Oh, I don't know,' Morris told him. "I know he'd take those four in front all right, but there were a couple horses behind me who looked like they coulda beat us all.'"

Then Davy went back to his newspaper.

IN ITS OBITUARY, the *Toronto Daily Star* called my father a 'noted handicapper', but the paper was being discreet, as newspapers were in those days. The writer surely knew that Davy had not only been a handicapper, he had also been one of Canada's top layoff artists. However, since he had never been charged or convicted—to handicap horses is legal, to lay off bets is not—it would have been libellous to print what everyone knew.

Laying off bets is as essential to the bookmaking business as re-insuring is to the insurance industry. The bookie and the insurance man are in the same boat. The insurance broker is happy to sell you earthquake coverage, an earthquake being a long shot. However, if there were an earthquake, the claims could bankrupt the company. To avoid this, the insurer takes out its own policy on your policy, thus spreading the risk. When a bookie does the same thing, it is called 'laying off'. The odds a bookie offers (or, these days, the point spread he offers) are designed to tempt bettors to take opposing positions, thereby balancing the book. But punters do not necessarily bet rationally. Torontonians may insistently pin their money, along with their hopes, on the Maple Leafs. If they do so in sufficient numbers, a Toronto bookie has a problem. He would like to stop taking bets on the Leafs, just in case they win. But if he does, he risks alienating his regular customers, and regular customers are the bookie's bread and butter. Regulars who bet irrationally are better customers still. So the bookie accepts all the bets he can, laying off to another bookie the action he cannot cover himself. That, however, may not be easy. If one bookie has heavy play on a horse or a team, chances are, so have the other bookies he knows. Enter the layoff artist.[1]

[1] Another way bookies would hedge their horse-racing bets was to bet 'comeback money'. Comeback money was money that, at the last minute, the bookie himself wagered through the pari-mutuel machines at the track, in order to lower the pay-

The man who developed the North American layoff system was Arnold Rothstein, also known as A.R., 'the Big Bankroll', and 'the King of the Gamblers'. Rothstein was a towering figure in the history of American organized crime. Arguably, he was the one who first organized it. Prior to Rothstein, gangsters worked their own turf; Rothstein accepted no such limit. Before Rothstein, the gangsters were beholden to the local political bosses; after Rothstein, the politicians were beholden to the gangsters. Arnold Rothstein, the man, wielded hitherto unprecedented power; Arnold Rothstein, the myth, wielded even more. He was the model for Meyer Wolfsheim in *The Great Gatsby*, for Nathan Detroit in *Guys and Dolls*, and for 'The Brain' in Damon Runyon's stories. His style served as the prototype for Hollywood gangsters and real gangsters alike. Said Charlie 'Lucky' Luciano, '[Rothstein] taught me how not to wear loud things but to have good taste; he taught me how to use knives and forks and things like that at the dinner table.... He was the best etiquette teacher a guy could ever have—real smooth.' Influential, Rothstein was; liked he was not. William J. Fallon, the famed Broadway lawyer, sneered, 'Rothstein is a man who dwells in doorways, a mouse standing in a doorway, waiting for his cheese.' Today, nearly a century after the fact, Rothstein is remembered as the man who fixed the 1919 World Series, though this may have been one of the few schemes of the era that he did not mastermind.[2]

out on the horse whose victory he feared. Only the top bookies, whose handle ran to four and five figures, could afford to make comeback bets, as it required a confederate at the race course with a bankroll in his pocket sufficient to shift the odds.

2 There is no consensus among biographers and historians as to what part, if any, Arnold Rothstein played in the 'Black Sox' scandal. Some claim Rothstein was the architect of the plot to throw the World Series, and the only man in America with the bankroll and the audacity to do it. Proponents of this theory dismiss evidence to the contrary as a clever alibi devised by Rothstein to cover his tracks. Others champion Rothstein's own account: he was approached to finance the scheme but refused, believing—correctly—that such a conspiracy could not be kept secret. Still, knowing the fix was in, A.R. bet heavily on the underdog Cincinnati Reds and won big. Investigations at the time were so marred by conflicting accounts, disappearing evidence, and delayed, bungled or incomplete police work that no one was ever convicted. Nonetheless, eight members of the losing Chicago White Sox, including star outfielder Shoeless Joe Jackson, were banned from baseball for life.

The King of the Gamblers was born in 1882, in New York City, the second son of a prominent Jewish businessman. He spent his early years uptown, safely distant from the teeming, squalid streets of the Lower East Side. Arnold's father, Abraham, was a successful clothing manufacturer, with a sterling reputation both within the Jewish community and without. After arbitrating a major dispute in the garment industry, Abraham Rothstein was nicknamed 'Abe the Just' by the Governor of New York State— an indication of the respect in which the elder Rothstein was held, and the anti-Semitism with which it was tinged. Abraham's oldest son continued on his father's high-minded path, entering the rabbinate. Arnold, the second son, went in the opposite direction.

Like Davy, Arnold had no use for his family's devout Judaism. His passion, from boyhood on, was gambling. Few, however, had Rothstein's facility for it. He had a head for figures and a gift for gauging probability. (In this way too, he and Davy were alike.) So, unlike most gamblers, Arnold tended to win. By the time he reached his teens, he was spending hours in the pool rooms, where the customers bet the horse-race 'pools'. He learned to shoot pool on the billiard tables that the pool-room operators had installed to keep the punters occupied between races. Rothstein was as skilled and focused with a cue as he was with cards or dice, and he quickly rose in the ranks of players and sharks. He would eventually play one of the most famous and most bet-upon matches in the history of the game, a thirty-four-hour marathon in John McGraw's pool room. Rothstein won.

Rothstein loved to gamble, in any form, but he loved one thing more: money. If Abe Orpen, Toronto's benevolent czar of gambling, was said to have 'played for the game and not the chips', A.R. was the opposite. Which game he played mattered little; his attention and his bankroll turned to anything that offered a high or a quick return. He ran floating crap games, black-tie casinos and bucket shops (fly-by-night stock-broking operations). He became a moneylender, an insurance agent, a bootlegger, a diamond merchant, an investor in Broadway shows, the owner of a racing stable, a labour racketeer, a real estate developer, and a heroin smuggler. Everything added to the bankroll, which Rothstein then used to back the next proposition. Every day, A.R. carried hundreds, and then thousands of dollars in cash in his pocket, so he could instantly finance others' schemes, most of them criminal. He would loan $100 to be repaid as $125 a week later. 'And,' he would add, 'God help

you if you don't.' Later he would insist the borrower take out life insurance from his insurance firm. His loan-sharking business was so extensive that in 1924 he was named the top-selling agent for the Norwalk Life Insurance Company.

Right from boyhood, Rothstein understood that money made money. Friday evenings, Arnold would steal the cash his father emptied from his pockets into a drawer for the Sabbath. Thus bankrolled, he would spend the night gambling, returning the money before his father opened the drawer again after sundown on Saturday. Arnold's father also had a prized, commemorative gold watch he kept in its hand-tooled leather case. He carried it only rarely, not wishing to be ostentatious. Arnold would steal the watch, pawn it for thirty dollars, and loan out the money at a usurious rate. When his customer paid off the debt he would redeem the watch from the pawnshop and return it to its case, until he needed it again.

I DOUBT THAT MY FATHER knew Arnold Rothstein personally. He was only twenty-three when Rothstein was killed in 1928, shot in an altercation over a gambling debt. Yet much of Davy's style reflected Rothstein's. He dressed in the natty way Rothstein did; like A.R., he always carried in his pocket a large roll of bills in a money clip; he kept his accounts in simple little black books, as Rothstein had famously done; and like A.R. he constantly conducted his business on the telephone.

Though few liked Rothstein, many, particularly Jews, admired his audacity, his chutzpah, Davy among them. Tales of Rothstein's exploits, his sangfroid and his cunning were recounted for years around backstretch kitchens, hotel barbershops and downtown delicatessens. There was, for example, the time A.R bet several thousand dollars that the train to Saratoga would pass more white horses than brown. It did—because Rothstein had arranged for a livery stable to deliver a string of white horses to a crossing en route.[3]

My father's favourite Rothstein story involved Peggy Hopkins Joyce, Broadway's most famous gold digger, and Percival H. Hill, the president of the American Tobacco Company. It offers a miniature portrait of how 'the Big Bankroll' got so big.

3 Another version of the story has John Bet-A-Million Gates as the perpetrator and Rothstein one of the victims.

Peggy Hopkins Joyce

In the 1910s, A.R. operated a small but well-appointed gambling club in a brownstone on West Forty-sixth Street, catering to wealthy clients who could afford to lose big, and then come back the next day to lose more. To attract such high rollers, Rothstein employed 'steerers', well-connected citizens who, for a fee, would lead their friends to his tables. The best steerers, Rothstein discovered, were the Broadway showgirls who, after the curtain fell, went out on the town with wealthy patrons.

A Ziegfeld girl named Peggy Hopkins was the most effective of the bunch.[4] The belle of Broadway at the time, Hopkins had no need to moonlight as a shill for a gambling joint, so Rothstein's recruiting effort was elaborate. He wooed her with roses and perfume, took her to dine at the best restaurants. Eventually he invited her to the races at Belmont Park, promising a pleasant and lucrative afternoon. Rothstein bet for his guest, with money he provided. But he refused to tell her which horse he had backed until the race was run, explaining, 'As soon as two people know a secret, eleven know it.' If this seemed odd or ungallant, Hopkins did not mind because, by the end of the afternoon, she was ahead over a thousand dollars.

Rothstein invited her back the next day, and she readily accepted. He held on to her bankroll. Once again, though her host's secrecy seemed excessive, she ended the day well ahead. They returned a third day and Hopkins' stake grew to over five thousand dollars. She asked Rothstein to cash her out, but he would not hear of it. He insisted they place one more bet on a sure winner who would be running later that afternoon. He was so confident, he intended to bet the whole five thousand. Hopkins tried to

4 Peggy Hopkins Joyce—her name after her third marriage—would become the most scandalous woman of the Jazz Age. She married the lumber magnate J. Stanley Joyce in 1920, the first of six millionaires she would marry and divorce. Her spending sprees were legendary, as were her lovers, among them Lee Shubert, Irving Thalberg, Walter Chrysler and Charlie Chaplin. Chaplin based his film 'A Woman of Paris' on Peggy Joyce. She appears in songs by Irving Berlin, Rodgers and Hart, and Cole Porter ('Should I make one man my choice / and regard divorce as treason / or should I, like Peggy Joyce / have a new one every season?') Despite having no musical or acting talent, Joyce starred in Broadway shows and Hollywood movies, including, in 1933, *International House* where she got top billing above W.C. Fields, Rudy Vallee, Bela Lugosi and George Burns and Gracie Allen.

dissuade him, but he waved off her fears. He did, however, tell her which race to watch for, and he agreed to inform her, once the betting had closed, which horse was theirs. When he did, she checked the Board: the horse was not one of the favourites. Hopkins watched nervously as the jockeys brought their mounts to the post. But then, to her delight, her horse broke from the gate in the lead and retained it as the furlongs passed. What Hopkins did not know was that this particular horse always started strong but then faded, finishing out of the money. And so it did once again. Hopkins cried in disappointment and chagrin. Rothstein commiserated. It is the nature of gambling, he explained, but he promised to make it up to her, in a way that involved no possibility of loss. The next time she was out on the town, he offered, she could bring her party to his club and he would give her 10 percent of any money her guests lost at the tables. Thus did Peggy Hopkins become Rothstein's steerer. It would prove fateful for them both, for not long after, Hopkins brought Rothstein a party that included the millionaire J. Stanley Joyce, whom she would marry; Bobbie Winthrop, a showgirl who would become Rothstein's longtime mistress; and Percival H. Hill, the president of the American Tobacco Company.

For Rothstein, Hill was a great catch, an amateur gambler of little skill and enormous wealth. As soon as he arrived, Hill headed for the roulette table, where he proceeded to lose $60,000, the biggest one-night loss by any one patron of Rothstein's club. But Hill was not done. He asked the pit boss for credit and a higher limit. The pit man went to A.R. It was not a simple decision. On the one hand, to cut Hill off would sully the establishment's reputation with its high-rolling clientele. On the other hand, the additional funds might allow Hill to recoup his losses. And there was a third consideration: if Hill continued to lose, would he honour his I.O.U.? There was no question that the president of the American Tobacco Company could afford to honour it but, in the cold light of day, would he do so? Rothstein made a quick decision. 'Mr Hill,' Rothstein told his guest, 'your credit is always good here, and the limit is yours to set. Good luck.'

By 4 a.m., Hill had lost $250,000 (over 3 million dollars today). 'My judgment has not been good tonight,' he announced, and said to Rothstein, 'If you will give me an I.O.U., I will sign it.' Rothstein gave him the paper. Hill wrote, 'Please pay to the bearer the above amount,' and affixed his signature. He instructed Rothstein to present the marker to Mr Sylvester, the treasurer of the American Tobacco Company. The note represented more

money than Rothstein had ever had up to that time—or it represented nothing, an uncollectable gambling debt.

The next morning Rothstein took a cab to the office of American Tobacco. He told the receptionist he was there to see Mr Sylvester at the request of Mr Hill. When asked what it was about, he said, 'It is personal.' He was admitted to the treasurer's suite, where he presented the I.O.U. Sylvester read the note and regarded Rothstein coldly. Then he said, 'This is a gambling debt, I presume. I doubt that it is collectable at law.'

'It is not my intention to go to law,' Rothstein replied.

Sylvester sat at his desk in silence while Rothstein stood. Finally he said, 'I am going to pay this. However, I am informing you now that I will not honour another such I.O.U., not even for five cents. Do we understand each other?' He was not looking for an answer. He ordered the cheque cut and dispatched a company representative to accompany Rothstein to the bank to facilitate the transaction. Without looking at Rothstein further, he dismissed him.

WITH THE MONEY HE WON from Hill and the many smaller amounts he collected from others—the same night Hill lost $250,000, Stanley Joyce lost $19,000—Rothstein was now in a position to start a new business in which he saw enormous potential: the layoff business. As a successful bookmaker himself, he well understood the need for a 'bank' to cover layoff bets. Now he had the capital to be that bank. Rothstein would take the bookies' excess action, but on his terms. If the horse paid 2 to 1, Rothstein would pay out at 8 to 5. The bookie could take Rothstein's price or leave it. Having little choice, the bookies took it. Soon calls and wires were coming in from bookmakers in Boston, Chicago and Kansas City. Rothstein was handling tens of thousands of dollars in layoff bets, then hundreds of thousands. He hired a smart young bookie named Frank Erickson to oversee the operation. As A.R. turned his attention to other corners of his empire, Erickson expanded the layoff business. Like his mentor, Erickson possessed a steel-trap mind, but unlike the cold, arrogant Rothstein, he had a sunny disposition and a generous nature. Everyone liked Frank Erickson, including my father, who had a favourite story about him.

Erickson was born in 1896 in Brighton Beach, a Jewish immigrant enclave on the Brooklyn waterfront. Many years later, when he appeared before the United States Senate's Crime Committee, Erickson neatly summed up his childhood.

'How far did your education progress?' Rudolph Halley, the committee counsel, asked him.

'About the fourth grade,' Erickson replied.

'And then what did you do? Did you go out to work?'

Erickson answered, 'I refuse to answer on the grounds that it might tend to incriminate me.'

The offending job was busing tables at Henderson's Music Hall at nearby Coney Island. One of the perks was the tip money the boys earned for running the waiters' and the patrons' bets to a nearby book. One day, as Erickson slipped out the back door with ten dollars to place on various horses, the manager caught him and ordered him back to wash dishes. The minutes ticked away; Erickson was stuck at the sink. Post time for the first race passed, and then it passed for the second race. When he finally was able to get away, Erickson ran to the book. In a cold sweat, he read the chalked-up results. To his relief, he discovered that most of the horses his customers had bet on had lost. Even after paying out the winners, he was left with more money than he earned in a week. Call it an epiphany. Erickson never looked back.

Frank Erickson turned Rothstein's layoff business into a coast-to-coast empire with agents in every major market. In Toronto, the man he chose was Davy Bossin.

• • • 7. Outward order and decency • • •

FOR MOST OF TWO decades, until 1939, Davy plied his legal and illegal trades without censure. How he managed that—by what combination of discretion, luck and payoffs—I simply do not know. Certainly the times were in his favour, for it was an era when the application of the law was at its most selective. William J. Gaynor, the Mayor of New York City, viewed things realistically when, back in 1910, he declared, 'The duty of the police is to preserve outward order and decency.'

In the 1920s and '30s, Toronto was a bastion of outward order and decency. While New York, Chicago and Montreal were rife with overt corruption and graft, Toronto appeared to live up to its reputation as Toronto the Good. The town had been populated in the mid-nineteenth century by Presbyterian Scots, who were followed by Protestant Irish. As it grew into a city, the founders' rectitude remained much in evidence. Even when I was a boy in the 1950s, the swings in Toronto's playgrounds were locked to their frames every Saturday night, so that no one could swing on them on Sunday. They were unlocked again Monday morning.

Toronto's shining code of public morality was decreed by its elected officials, but its enforcement fell to the police. In the 1930s they were hard men, the cops as hard as the robbers—men like Sgt. Frank 'Rubber Hose' Crow, who did not earn his nickname fighting fires. Or Sgt. Bill Nursey, who liked to walk behind the men he arrested, stepping on their heels with the toes of his boots. By the time Nursey's prisoners got to City Hall, they were unable to walk and would have to be dragged to the cells. By William Gaynor's definition, the Toronto police did their duty well: outward order and decency prevailed. Inward order was more problematic and, for the most part, its failings went unreported.

So I was fortunate to meet Herb Thurston in 1998, when he was eighty-six. Thurston had been a Toronto cop for forty years, from 1936 to 1976, ending his career as a member of the Ontario Police Commission. By the time I interviewed him, a year before his death, cancer had taken his vocal cords and he spoke by holding an artificial larynx to his throat. No matter: he talked for hours. Herb sounded like a robot amplified by an

electric razor, but his stories of policing Toronto the Good were worth every hour it took to decipher what I had taped.

HERB THURSTON was an unlikely prospect for a policeman. He was born in 1912 and grew up shooting craps with Max Bluestein, who would become one of Toronto's most notorious loan sharks and gambling operators. Herb was an excellent crap shooter himself, which he demonstrated during his police training. One lunchtime, his fellow cadets started up a friendly game, using the confiscated dice their instructor had displayed in a class on gambling offences. Herb cleaned them out. It was a story James Mackie, Toronto's Chief of Police from 1958 to 1970, loved to tell about the man who, by then, headed the force's morality squad.

Thurston would not have become a cop but for another of his youthful talents, the pole vault. In those days, the Police Games were a major annual event in Toronto; when the police from Detroit came to town to challenge Toronto's finest, the meet filled Varsity Stadium. The Toronto team needed a pole vaulter. It was 1936, the middle of the Depression, and Herb Thurston needed a job.

The new recruit was thin as a rail and, once he joined the force, as straight as an arrow. His police classmates called him Fearless Fosdick, after the comic-strip character he resembled in both physique and uprightness. Jocko Thomas, the longtime police reporter for the *Toronto Star*, recalled a Sunday when Thurston hid behind a telephone pole—he was that thin—and then pounced on him when Jocko came out of a store with a pack of cigarettes he had purchased on the Sabbath, in contravention of Ontario's strict Lord's Day code. Herb had nothing against Thomas nor, for that matter, against the bookies; he grew up with them. His father was a horse player and Herb had often been with him while he placed his bets. But when he became a cop, he became a cop.

Fearless Fosdick was not, however, a role model for everyone on the force. 'One day,' Thurston told me, 'right after I graduated from the police academy, I was walking my new beat along Queen Street. I was green as the grass. I had just been assigned to Number 3 Division, which covered the west side of downtown. It was lunchtime and I was headed back to the station when I bumped into a friend from school.'

Thurston and his friend stopped to talk but, unbeknownst to them, the store in front of which they lingered was a book. This was less coincidental than it sounds; in those days, Queen Street was chock-a-block with

bookmakers. They used to say that on a hot day when the bookies had their windows open, you could walk along Queen and hear an entire race broadcast without missing a furlong.

Since it was lunchtime, a steady stream of punters headed to the shop to place their bets, but seeing a cop at the door, they veered off. After a few minutes, the proprietor came out and told Thurston, 'Get the hell out of here! You are ruining my business!' Thurston bristled, and the bookie went on, 'Listen, kid, if you are not getting your share, talk to Henry and Baker.'

When Thurston got back to the station, the detectives already knew about the encounter. 'They said they were working on something big,' Thurston recalled. 'They told me to report back to them if I saw anything, all that bullshit. So I went back every day at lunchtime, and counted the people going in and out, and reported it. I did that for three days. On the fourth day, I was transferred out of the division.'

On another occasion, in those early days of Thurston's career, an instruction came down from Toronto's chief magistrate, 'Honest' Bob Brown: there was to be a crackdown on drunk driving. There were to be no more friendly, out-of-court settlements. That night, Thurston arrested a drunk in an expensive roadster. 'I booked him and, the next morning, went to City Hall to give evidence at the arraignment.' But there was no arraignment. The court clerk, a retired cop, saw the young policeman's perplexity and asked him, 'Do you have a case here, sonny?' Thurston gave him the name of the man he had arrested. The clerk checked the calendar and said, 'No such arrest.' Thurston told him he had collared the man himself. 'Just a minute,' said the clerk.

When he returned, he told Herb the case had been settled out of court. 'It can't be,' Herb replied, 'we just got a bloody order from Magistrate Brown!' The old cop looked at him and said, 'It's Magistrate Brown who settled it.'

'I said, "He can't do that!"' Thurston told me. 'And he said, "You want to go see His Honour?" I said, "You bet I do." The old cop just smiled. He took me down the hall, and rapped on the door to Bob Brown's chambers. That was the first time I ever saw him. He had a rose in his lapel. He said to me, "You're a fine-looking policemen, how long you been on?" I told him, and he said, "Son, the driver of that car is a very prominent man, and his career would be finished if this became public, so I settled it out of court." I said, "But you just gave us a directive," and he said, "Do you like being a policeman?"'

'That's just the way things were.'

J.E. Jones was another Toronto magistrate in the 1930s. The *Star's* Jocko Thomas told me Magistrate Jones was widely known as the man to see to dispose of summonses for minor infractions. Jones had published a hymn book and kept a stack of them by the door of his chambers. To show their gratitude, Jones's petitioners bought hymnals on their way out.

Such accommodations, at least for the right people, were common. Occasionally there was a scandal, as in 1933, when Toronto's spit-and-polish Chief Constable, Brigadier-General Dennis Draper, personally ordered the withdrawal of a drunk-driving charge against the son of a federal cabinet minister. The city council demanded Draper's resignation, but Draper was well-connected with the Conservative Party. He kept his post for another thirteen years.

Everyone I spoke to who remembered Toronto in the 1930s had a story or two like these, but only Herb Thurston seemed to care. Cronyism and graft were expected in civic life, and Torontonians were satisfied that the graft was only in pockets, even if those pockets were bulging. So the fact that Playfair Brown's horse room operated for years directly across the street from the mayor's office window was accepted with a shrug. Brown was, after all, superintendent of an Anglican Sunday school.

'There were some cozy arrangements between the bookmakers and some of the politicians and the police and even the magistrates, including Honest Bob Brown,' according to Thurston. The officials, like everyone else, liked to play the horses. But they got a special deal from the bookies: when they won, they collected; when they lost, the bets were forgiven. Each week, a different bookmaker carried this complimentary action, so the cost was distributed fairly across the industry.

I don't know if my father was in on that, or some other payoff scheme, or if that contributed to his seeming immunity from prosecution. It is possible that Davy's extraordinary caution was protection enough. He was, for an outlaw, singularly circumspect. He wrote no betting slips, keeping track of everything in his head. He always paid in cash. His office was a room in the Royal York Hotel, so his phone calls were routed through the hotel's switchboard, making them difficult to trace. And, when the weather was good, he would walk the five miles from our house to the Royal York with a pocketful of change, stopping at phone booths and making calls along the way. Thus he laid off bets worth hundreds of thousands of dollars to New York and Chicago, for years, and never got busted. Not for that.

• • • 8. The race wire • • •

HAD DAVY STUCK to the layoff business, he might have lived his whole life peacefully outside the law. However, sometime in the mid-1930s he decided to go straight, or at least straighter. Davy now offered instantaneous race information to horse players; the voice heard along Queen Street calling the races may well have been Davy's. On the surface of it, that would seem a mild transgression and, indeed, it fell into a legal grey area, but that was the crime for which the authorities would relentlessly pursue Davy from 1939 to 1945. Their vehemence had little to do with what Davy actually did—taking the coded race accounts off the telegraph wire and calling them out over the telephone. But the Crown considered that act to be the key to a continent-wide criminal conspiracy. This was a delusion, but the theory gripped the imagination of police and politicians across the continent as the 1930s came to an end.

According to the cops, the trouble started with the advent of the telegraph. In that respect—the significance of the telegraph to the gambling business—the cops were completely right: nowhere did the telegraph have greater impact than on horse-race gambling, which it turned into a continent-wide industry. Before the wires went up in the latter part of the nineteenth century, all conversations, including those that ended in bets, were local. News travelled only as fast as a man could carry it. But with the telegraph, information travelled instantly anywhere the telegraph wires went. And among the first places the wires were strung were the racetracks. Western Union stationed some of its first telegraphers at the tracks, where they tapped out race results as soon as the horses crossed the finish line. From the beginning, the fees Western Union (and later AT&T) received from its racetrack operations provided a big chunk of the company's income. For who had greater need of timely information than punters and their bookies? Now, for the first time, both bookies and bettors could know immediately where they stood. Had they won big or lost big on the first race? Knowing the answer, they could bet the next race accordingly, and the next and the next. And they could now do so apprised of all the last-minute changes in odds, jockeys and track conditions—information

that also came over the wire. The bookies' handle (the total bets on an event) skyrocketed.

Even more important to the burgeoning industry, the telegraph extended the betting season. The few weeks when local race meetings were held had been a brief spree for gamblers; now, playing the ponies could be a year-round occupation. When the races ended in Ontario and the horses moved on to Maryland, Florida or California, all a punter needed to continue trying his luck was a copy of the *Daily Racing Form* and the results off the wire.

The race wire, as the system of telegraphed racing information came to be called, created not just a gambling industry; it created a leisure industry, an early form of remote entertainment—before radio. With news flashing in from the tracks all afternoon, more and more punters spent those afternoons at their bookie's, enjoying the conviviality along with the gambling. Bookie joints expanded into horse rooms, with all the appurtenances of the track except the horses. Announcers would call the races, furlong by furlong, as the telegraphed account came in. Later, in my father's day, the information was passed on by telephone, and the call could be amplified for the benefit of the patrons—which is how Davy's voice could be heard through the open windows of the bookie joints along Queen Street.

For those who opposed gambling, the industrialization the telegraph brought to bookmaking was deeply discouraging. Reformers were appalled at the fast-spreading appeal of playing the horses. One 'uplifter' selflessly attended a horse room and reported, 'It is a terrible spectacle. Men and women, boys and girls, as if bewitched, yell, call for their horses to win, scream out in their excitement, snap their fingers and jump up and down, and the race being run a thousand miles or more away!' Foes of gambling pressured Western Union to stop the telegraph, 'this noble discovery', from being put 'to base and hurtful use'.[1]

By 1904, the reformers had mounted sufficient pressure to force Western Union to curtail its racetrack transmissions. However, as would be the case with Prohibition, all that really changed was who got paid for providing the service. The stream of racing news continued unabated, with new entrepreneurs leasing Western Union's lines and hiring their own tele-

1 Current debate about online gambling and pornography is a reprise of a song first sung about the race wire.

```
..ADD ENTRIES...GARDEN STATE ENTRIES.....TRACK GOOD...POST    PN.....FIRST RACE....
   .              .    .                    .          .230.            .
      CLNG.. YO UP...SIX FURS...                        CNG OUT.
   .1100.    4..      .        16.....                         ..  .    .....
      NY IS    IS   NEAR POST        NY IS EVEN.        NY FILED
      2  8...16 12.    .   .....     10 .     ....      .  .    53½.....
      QTR A HF... BY TWO...          AT HALF... A HF... A HF...
      16 .    10 .    13.....          46 .    15 .    12.....
      STCH... A LG... A HF...       SALES... GREY SQUIRE BY A LG... BRAINSTORM...
         15 .    16 .   12.....       15  .       .   .   12          16
   LITTLE FLYER.           NY OK GREY SQUIRE...BRAINSTORM...LITTLE FLYER...TIME  NEXT
      .    .......   .  .  .  .                                          127    20
                                  NUTS
                              ..  11.30...530...410...40.10...17.60...600..
```

Race wire ticker tape. Reading from this coded account, Davy would have
called the race like this: 'Those are the entries for the first race at Garden
State. The track is good. Post time is 2:30. The first race is a claiming race for
a purse of $1100, for horses 4 years or older, 6 furlongs, 16 horses entered...
The horses are now coming onto the track.... Odds on the number 2 horse,
Club Flush, have dropped to 8 to 1. The odds on number 16, Little Flyer, are
now 12 to 1.... The horses are approaching the starting post, and the
favourite, number 10, Country Cousin, is now even money.... They are at
the post, and they are off at exactly 2:53:30.... At the quarter, it's number 16,
Little Flyer, by a half length, followed by number 10, Country Cousin, two
lengths ahead of Broiled Brisket, number 13 in third place... At the half, it is
still Little Flyer by half a length. Grey Squire, number 15, has moved up to
second place, a half length ahead of number 12, Brainstorm.... And as they
round the final turn Grey Squire has taken the lead, a length ahead of Little
Flyer who has dropped back to second, a half length ahead of Brainstorm
who continues to gain. And the winner is Grey Squire by a length, Brain-
storm is second and Little Flyer third, all unofficial.... The New York result
is now official.... The winning time, one minute, 27 seconds. The next race
will be off at 3:20.... Grey Squire paid $11.30 to win, $5.30 to place and $4.10
to show. Brainstorm paid $40.10 to place and $17.50 to show. Little Flyer
paid $6.00 to show.'

graph operators. The most successful and far-sighted of these service
providers was a former Western Union telegrapher named John Payne.
The Payne Telegraph Service of Cincinnati sold race information to book-
makers in cities scattered across the eastern and central United States.

Payne's biggest customer was Mont Tennes, a Chicago gangster who used the wire to gain primacy over his rivals. In 1907, for a payment of three hundred dollars a day, Tennes acquired the exclusive right to distribute Payne's information in Illinois. The wire proved so vital to Chicago's bookies that Tennes was able to raise the price he charged for the service to an onerous 50 percent of the bookie's earnings. If a bookie balked, Tennes, whose thuggery was notorious, employed other means of persuasion. Soon he ruled over most of the gambling in Chicago. Then, in 1909, he turned his persuasive powers back on John Payne. After his home was bombed, Payne sold out to Tennes, and Mont Tennes became the proprietor of the race wire, which he renamed the General News Bureau. The wire now extended through much of the United States.

For the next eighteen years, Tennes beat back all challenges to his gambling empire, whether from the law or the lawless. In one three-month period, his home and his office were bombed six times. Tennes retaliated in kind. The 'Gambling War', as it was called in the press, repelled enough Chicagoans that they elected reformers to city and state office, but Tennes continued to control the police force and thus weather the wave of reform.

It would be another decade before Mont Tennes finally met his match. In 1927, Al Capone was a twenty-eight-year-old bootlegger who had made a fortune smuggling Canadian liquor into the American Midwest. Scarface Al's reputation for brutality exceeded even that of Mont Tennes. The aging gambling boss opted for retirement, ceding to Capone his bookmaking empire.

But not the General News Bureau. That he offered to Moses Annenberg, a self-made tycoon who owned, among other newspapers, enterprises and properties, the *Daily Racing Form*. Annenberg's son and others close to him advised him against taking up the race wire, with its sordid history and underworld ties. Annenberg, however, was intrigued, seeing the potential for a monopoly on all racing information, print and electronic, throughout North America. He went ahead and bought a controlling interest in the General News Bureau. Then he proceeded to buy out, or force out, almost all competing race-wire services until he had, effectively, the monopoly he had envisioned. The man he got to front his Toronto outlet was a prominent figure in Ontario gambling named Sam Roher. To run the operation, Roher hired one of the city's senior layoff artists, Davy Bossin.

ONE SUMMER AFTERNOON in the early 1970s, I ate lunch at the United Bakers Dairy Restaurant. The *milshike* (no meat) delicatessen had been a fixture of Toronto's Jewish community since it opened in 1912, when three kosher bakers pooled their money and started a lunch counter near Eaton's clothing factory in the heart of the Ward. Eight years later, the UBDR moved to Spadina Avenue, following its customers as they abandoned the Ward for the row houses a few blocks west. The restaurant opened its new doors in 1920, and there it stayed for the next sixty-four years until it moved north when the Spadina-area Jews left the inner city for the suburbs. There the UBDR continues to this day, operated by the grandchildren of one of the original bakers.

In the 1970s, when I ate there from time to time, the United Bakers Dairy Restaurant was still on Spadina Avenue, under a pressed-tin ceiling. Below was all fluorescent light and Formica. The waitresses were grouchy and the counter man was as old as Methuselah. One day as I paid my bill, I asked him how long he had lived in Toronto. '*Lenger vi mayne tseyn,*' he said. Longer than my teeth.

So I asked him, 'Did you know the Bossins?'

'Sure,' he said, 'I knew the Bossins. I knew Hye, the *schreiber.* I knew Celia, Sady, Bessie...'. He proceeded to list my father's numerous siblings and cousins. 'I knew Art. I knew Davy...'.

'Davy was my father,' I told him.

'Sure, I knew Davy. We used to call him Davy the Punk.'

'Davy the Punk?' I had never heard that. 'Why did you call him Davy the Punk?'

'Because he was a *farbrecher*. He was a gangster.'

SINCE THAT CONVERSATION, I have come across two other references to Davy the Punk, one in a list of colourful racetrack nicknames recalled by the sports writer Jim Coleman. But the most intriguing mention came via my cousin, David Bossin, my father's namesake. David was born in 1925 and lived in Palm Desert, California, now a suburb of Palm Springs. Palm Springs is one of the wealthiest communities in the world with streets named after its prominent citizens, among them Dinah Shore, Gerald Ford and Bob Hope. On Frank Sinatra Drive is the Annenberg Golf Course. The course is named after Walter, the celebrated son, not Moses, his notorious father.

For most of his father's life, Walter Annenberg was a charming but feckless playboy. However, upon Moses Annenberg's imprisonment and death, responsibility for the family's publishing and other enterprises fell to Walter. He quickly grew into the job; he raised the Annenberg stable of publications to new heights, in part by creating special interest magazines like *Seventeen* and *TV Guide*. He built television stations, starting in 1948. (His first was only the fifteenth TV station licensed in the United States.) Where Moses Annenberg, the father, was shunned as a racketeer, Walter, the son, hobnobbed with Queen Elizabeth, Ronald Reagan, Gerald Ford and Richard Nixon. Nixon appointed him ambassador to the Court of St. James's. Walter became, as well, one of America's foremost philanthropists, funding, among many charities and institutions, the A.M. Annenberg Schools of Communication at the University of Pennsylvania and the University of California. He named the schools after his father.

Walter lived like a squire on a vast Palm Springs estate called Sunnylands. On one occasion, my cousin David visited Sunnylands for a charity function hosted by the Annenbergs. As David went through the receiving line, Walter Annenberg noticed David's name tag. 'I once knew a Dave Bossin,' he said to David, 'up in Canada. He was called Davy the Punk.' Annenberg chuckled and David moved on. My cousin had no way to know the significance of the admission, or that Walter Annenberg's father had paid a terrible price to cover up the fact that Walter had known people like Davy the Punk.

• • • 9. Annenberg • • •

THOUGH THEY MET only occasionally, Moses Annenberg changed the
course of my father's life. He did this twice, once when Davy became the
General News Bureau's manager in Toronto, and a second time when
Annenberg so provoked America's highest authorities that they unleashed
a campaign against him that jumped the borders of the United States and
swept Davy up too.

Moses Annenberg was born in a barren East Prussian village in 1877.
Seven years later, literally a shoeless child, he emigrated with his mother
and siblings to Chicago. Moses' father had come to America three years
earlier, and now the re-united family settled in the Patch, Chicago's notori-
ous tenderloin district.

Moe Annenberg's early years were much like Davy's in Toronto. Like
Davy, he was out of school and on the streets by twelve, and he too had no
time for his parents' Old World Judaism. Like Davy, Moe worked around
horses from an early age, in Annenberg's case in a livery stable. Like my
uncles Hye and Art, he took up boxing, a skill he practised on the street
and in the saloon. Annenberg worked at a variety of jobs until 1900 when,
at twenty-three, he followed his older brother Max into the circulation
department of William Randolph Hearst's upstart newspaper the *Chicago
American*. This put Moe in the thick of Chicago's 'circulation war', in
which the city's competing newspapers fought viciously for street-corner
sales. The *American*, the *Tribune* and the *Daily News* all employed gangs of
toughs to intimidate the news vendors into selling their paper exclusively.
Twenty-seven newsies were killed and hundreds injured. Moe ran one of
the gangs for the *American*, hiring his old street-brawling pals. His fight-
ing, leadership and organizational skills impressed both his comrades and
his bosses and he was soon promoted. Annenberg rose rapidly through the
circulation side of the Hearst organization. In a few years he became the
leading newspaper and magazine distributor in the Midwest. In 1917 he
published his first paper, the *Wisconsin News*. Five years later, he bought
the *Daily Racing Form*.

Moses Annenberg was not a racing buff, but he saw that millions of

Moses Annenberg

other people were, and that many of them placed their bets on the basis of the information the *Racing Form* provided. So he purchased the historic little paper, first published in 1894, and turned it into the horse-player's Bible, covering every horse, in every race, at every track in North America. He did this by printing seven different editions simultaneously in seven cities, among them Toronto. These multiple, regional editions were a radical publishing innovation in the early 1920s. Meanwhile, Moe bought out, out-performed, or simply strong-armed the publishers of other racing papers, until he had a virtual monopoly. Then he bought the controlling interest in the General News Bureau from Mont Tennes, and set about swallowing up the competing wire services as well.

Moses Annenberg was not a gangster, even though he would later be tarred with that brush; to the extent he is remembered nowadays, it is that inaccurate notoriety that has stuck. In fact, Annenberg was a typical capitalist of his era, hard-nosed, unscrupulous, and not above judicious use of violence. But those were secondary attributes of Moe's business acumen. Primarily his success arose from his quick-wittedness and prescience. For instance, in 1913, he was casting about for a gimmick to boost newspaper circulation. He knew that when his '40-mile men' (subscription salesmen) knocked on a door, it was mostly women who answered. So one evening, sitting in the kitchen with his family, Annenberg asked his wife what women run out of most often.

'Teaspoons,' she replied.

'That's it!' Annenberg exclaimed to his children. 'Little Woman has just made us a fortune.'

Indeed, 'Little Woman'—as Moses called Sadie Annenberg—had. Moe immediately started a business manufacturing teaspoons decorated with the crests of American states and Canadian provinces. He then convinced newspapers across the continent to offer the spoons as a subscription bonus—newspaper subscribers could redeem a new one each week for 15 cents. He sold over a billion spoons and collected a royalty on each one.

IN THE 1930S, when my father operated the Toronto terminus of Annenberg's race wire, he did not work for Annenberg, not officially. But the independence was nominal. Officially, the *Canadian Racing and Financial News*, as the Toronto business was called, was merely a subscriber to Annenberg's news service. However, the monthly charge for Moe's information was determined by the profit the Toronto operation made, and

Annenberg visited from time to time to check the books. Walter Annenberg, who went everywhere with his father, no doubt knew Davy the Punk from these visits.

The *Canadian Racing and Financial News*, or the 'Scratch Sheet' as it was known to the racing crowd, operated out of a former rooming house on Mercer Street, in the Ward. A few hundred copies of the paper (two foolscap sheets, printed on both sides) were run off every morning on a Gestetner machine in the basement of the building. Above, on the ground floor, there were eighteen telephone consoles, at which operators sat in the afternoons, answering customers' requests for race results. Upstairs, on the second floor, a telegrapher decoded the Morse code feed off the wire and dictated the messages to a stenographer.[1] She passed the information to Davy, who sat at a fifty-six-line telephone switchboard. At a desk across the room sat Sam Roher, the official owner of the *Canadian Racing and Financial News*.

The Scratch Sheet sold at newsstands around Toronto for a quarter. It offered the morning's racing news—the morning line, scratches, jockeys, weights and so on. But its real value was that it included a daily code number. With the code, the purchasers could phone for the results anytime after a race was run. The eighteen 'telephone girls' would answer the customers' questions using the numbers corresponding to listings in the Scratch Sheet. My mother was one of the telephone girls one day, filling in for someone who called in sick. But numbers were never my mother's strong suit. She kept mixing up the codes, and was not asked to fill in again.

In addition, the Scratch Sheet offered a more exclusive service. It was the heart of the business, and it was what my father did at his switchboard. For a hefty fee, a bookie could become one of the fifty subscribers Davy called every day except Sunday. He did this by plugging a connector cable into the switchboard and dialling the first five digits of the subscriber's number. (At the time, Toronto phone numbers were six digits long. The first five digits selected the particular customer's phone; the last digit rang it.) Before Davy dialled the last digit, he plugged in the next customer, and began dialling him. This process was then repeated for each of his subscribers. When all fifty were plugged in, Davy dialed the final digit of their numbers. As the phones rang, and the customers picked up, they were

1 In later years, the information came in on ticker tape.

connected to Davy's switchboard. By this method, my father jerry-rigged a one-way conference call and reported to fifty customers at once. All afternoon, he kept the phone line open, effectively broadcasting the racing news from across North America live to his subscribers. He reported the fluctuating odds; he called the races, furlong by furlong; he announced the exact starting times (to the second) so bookies could not be 'past-posted'—tricked into accepting a last-minute bet by someone who already knew the result. What the stock ticker was to a stock-broker, Davy's open phone line was to the bookies.

MY FATHER was a cynical man. He rarely expressed admiration for anybody, but he admired Moses Annenberg, taking delight in his de facto boss's shrewdness and *chutzpah*. That is what shines through the two stories I remember Davy telling about Moses Annenberg.

The first took place sometime around 1930, when one of Annenberg's wire-service competitors, the Greater New York Wire Service (GNYWS), bribed a telegraph employee to tap into the line carrying Annenberg's General News Bureau signal from Chicago to New York. The GNYWS was owned by Waxey Gordon, a notorious New York gangster of the 1920s. Having tapped Annenberg's transmission, GNYWS then forwarded the bootlegged race results to its own customers' bookmaking operations, sparing Gordon the cost of gathering his own information.

Annenberg found out about Waxey Gordon's wiretap. At first he did nothing, but one afternoon when he had all the pieces in place for an elaborate sting, he delayed sending the live account of one of the races over the line to New York—the line that Gordon's outfit had tapped. (Annenberg passed on the race results to his own New York customers by phone.) While Gordon's bookies were still waiting for the race to start, Annenberg sent runners to the GNYWS-serviced books, where they placed heavy, last-minute bets on the horse they knew had already won. A few minutes later, Annenberg turned the signal back on, and the hapless bookies discovered that they had lost thousands of dollars to the lucky last-minute bettors. Then, in a brilliant stratagem, Moe had his agents return to the books they had swindled at closing time. Annenberg's men gave back the bookies' money and explained what had occurred—and how it could happen again if the bookies continued to rely on Waxey Gordon's unreliable, second-hand information. The bookmakers quickly switched to Annenberg's service.

Waxey Gordon Frank Nitti

The other Annenberg story Davy told took place a half-dozen years later, in 1935. By that time, Moe wanted to rid himself of his junior partners in the General News Bureau. (Mont Tennes had sold Moses the controlling share, but had sold smaller pieces of the business to others.) The partners, who were prospering under Moe's management, refused to sell out. So Annenberg started a new, competing company, the Nation-Wide News Service, of which he was sole proprietor. Nation-Wide then proceeded to offer an identical service at deep-discount prices. Annenberg watched cheerfully as General News' customers switched allegiance. GNB sank into debt, and the value of his partners' shares plummeted. Of course, so did Annenberg's, but his profits from Nation-Wide compensated for his losses at General News. Moe's partners sued him, citing a litany of Annenberg's unscrupulous tactics, none of which he disputed. Instead his lawyer, Weymouth Kirkland, one of Chicago's top attorneys, argued that the General News Bureau was, de facto, a criminal enterprise abetting bookies in their unlawful trade. Kirkland reminded the judge that the courts could not be used to divide the spoils of crime, a common-law tenet dating back to 1725, when an English judge refused to arbitrate between highwaymen in a dispute over their respective shares of their loot. The Chicago judge ruled for Annenberg, and the decision was upheld on appeal. Annenberg got away with it.

My father's version of the story ended there, amid laughter, but the reality did not. One of the junior partners in General News was Jack Lynch, a confidant of the Capone Mob. Al Capone was by then in prison and the gang was under the control of Capone's lieutenants, one of whom was Frank 'the Enforcer' Nitti. At Lynch's urging, Nitti visited Annenberg and suggested they become 'partners' in the wire-service business. Moe

demurred, but when an assassin narrowly missed shooting him, he reconsidered, and sent Nitti $100,000 in hundred-dollar bills. ('Bobby,' my father would say, 'a Smith and Wesson beats four aces.') Annenberg and his family hastily retreated to Florida, where he lived under the protection of his old friend and sometime colleague Meyer Lansky. Lansky brokered a deal with Nitti, purportedly for a million dollars, after which the Capone Mob left Annenberg alone.

BY THIS TIME Annenberg was nearing sixty. He was one of the richest men in America. He began to think about his legacy and, in particular, what he would leave to his son, Walter. As if in answer to a prayer, one of the oldest American newspapers, the *Philadelphia Inquirer*, went up for sale. Moe snapped it up.

Like most wealthy Americans, Annenberg was a Republican, and he turned the *Inquirer* into a shrill critic of President Roosevelt and his New Deal, or 'Raw Deal' as the *Inquirer* took to calling it. Moe also used the paper to attack and unseat the Governor of Pennsylvania, a prominent Democrat. Annenberg was becoming a force in national politics, but in doing so he made himself an enemy, a man who was more powerful and more implacable than the Capone mob.

Beneath Franklin Delano Roosevelt's avuncular image was as ruthless a foe as Frank Nitti. The 1940 presidential election loomed, and Roosevelt wanted Annenberg silenced. 'I want Moe Annenberg for dinner,' the President told his Secretary of the Treasury, Henry Morgenthau. 'You are going to have him for breakfast—fried,' Morgenthau answered.[2]

Morgenthau ordered government tax accountants to audit Annenberg's business empire for tax evasion—the strategy that had brought down Al Capone, Waxey Gordon and other gangsters whom the law had been unable to convict for anything else. After a year's work, the auditors still could not untangle Moe's myriad interlocking companies and investments, and they might never have done so had not nineteen boxes of Annenberg's private financial records been misdelivered, sent not to Moe's private office but to the office of the government's investigators. With the

2 In a lifelong effort to rehabilitate his father's reputation, Walter Annenberg unearthed memos, letters and diaries that revealed how Roosevelt and his inner circle had orchestrated Moses' downfall.

new information the auditors presented a case to Roosevelt's Attorney General, Frank Murphy. They believed they now had the evidence to successfully prosecute. Whether they were right remains a matter of speculation. The strength of the government's case was never tested.

In a brilliant if unscrupulous move, Murphy charged Moe's son Walter with tax evasion, along with his father. The prosecutors knew that Walter had nothing to do with Annenberg's tax preparations. But they also knew that Moses Annenberg was devoted to his family, particularly to his only son. They calculated that Moses would do anything to keep Walter's name from being dragged through the mud. They were right: in return for having the charges dropped against Walter, Moe pleaded guilty. He agreed to pay $1,217,296 in back taxes and another $9.5 million in penalties—well over a hundred million in today's dollars. It was the largest tax evasion fine ever paid.

That, however, was insufficient restitution for the White House. 'I want him behind bars,' Roosevelt told Attorney General Murphy, who assigned the case to James Wilkerson, the judge who had sentenced Al Capone to eleven years' imprisonment for his unpaid taxes. Annenberg's plea bargain notwithstanding, Wilkerson insisted on hearing evidence to determine his sentence.

To prosecute, the Justice Department chose a young staff lawyer named William Campbell, who performed his duties zealously. 'I'll give you the names of three people that Annenberg has had killed in the city of Chicago in the last five years,' Campbell exclaimed at one point. In fact, he had no evidence of the crimes, and there were no charges, not even a credible allegation. However, such legal niceties did not stand in the way of *The United States v. Moses Annenberg*. Judge Wilkerson was as partisan as Campbell. One day, he took the young prosecutor aside and told him, 'Tell the Attorney General ... if he wants to tell me privately, or through you, of a recommendation, I will do my best to follow his recommendation. I'm all for you, my boy.'

In the end, in addition to the millions of dollars he had already agreed to pay, Annenberg was sentenced to three years in prison. 'Certainly the law does not demand as satisfaction that this man be completely broken and destroyed,' Weymouth Kirkland argued for his client, but that was precisely what the most powerful men in the United States demanded.

Once in prison, Annenberg was singled out for abusive treatment, with the enthusiastic approval of a notoriously anti-Semitic warden. Then,

despite Annenberg's deteriorating health, the White House intervened with the parole Board to prevent his parole. Medical help that would have perhaps lengthened his life, and certainly would have made his last years more comfortable, was denied. Only when he was near death from a brain tumour was Moe Annenberg released. He died a month later, on July 20, 1942. His last words were whispered to his son. 'Walter,' he said, 'who knows what is the scheme of things. My suffering has all been for the purpose of making you a man.'

'His mistreatment was the making of me,' Walter would say. It was also the making of the young prosecutor, William Campbell. Two months after the trial, he was named a federal judge. A few months later, Judge Wilkerson was awarded 'senior status'—retirement at full pay. Attorney General Murphy was promoted to the Supreme Court. In 1940, Roosevelt was re-elected to an unprecedented third term as President.

'The tremendous injustice to your father has been on my mind, on and off, for years,' William Hopewell, one of the government auditors on the Annenberg case, wrote to Walter Annenberg in 1981. 'I am sure that he was not guilty as charged.' Without a doubt, Moses Annenberg was indeed the victim of a 'tremendous injustice', but he could not fairly be called an *innocent* victim. Though Prosecutor Campbell could not have named the three people he claimed Annenberg had killed in Chicago (as no such killings had occurred), Moses was no stranger to strong-arm tactics. He had, over the years, turned a blind eye when his lieutenants employed them. He had used his newspapers and his wealth to buy elections for candidates who would do his bidding. He had cheated massively on his taxes. But these were common practices among the industrialists of the time, and they were not what brought Annenberg down. His real crime was attempting to go straight.

Moses Annenberg overreached. Having bought and sold politicians, having employed Philadelphia lawyers to manipulate the judicial system, and having outsmarted all the rivals he had encountered, Annenberg was flushed with his own success. Arnold Rothstein had wielded enormous power to corrupt and influence, but always from a back room; Annenberg attempted to come around and enter through the front door. To those on the inside, that was intolerable. They cut him down to size.

Like Moses Annenberg, my father had little regard for men in positions of power. And as with Annenberg, the authorities would pursue him relentlessly, albeit with a Canadian reverence for law, or the appearance of

law. Davy's prosecution was small-scale compared with Annenberg's, commensurate with the life he led. Unlike his boss, Davy was neither ambitious nor flamboyant. This was not only a matter of discretion. He simply was not a man who cared to be rich or famous or powerful. Davy liked simple things—a good musical, a good story, *kibitzing* with his pals. There was a robin's nest under the eave of our neighbour's roof when I was growing up. It could be viewed from our back door. Davy could stand there watching the robins for an hour. In the end, I think that is what kept him out of jail. His silence, his patience, his satisfaction with the modest joys of ordinary life would stand him in good stead. And as the 1930s drew to a close, staying out of jail would take all the resources my father could muster. For the wake from the frenzied pursuit of Moses Annenberg was about to sweep across Lake Ontario and break on its Canadian shore.

10. An expert on horses

I LOVE THE INTERNET. Every back issue of the *Globe and Mail* and the *Toronto Star* is now available on line, searchable from home. Typing in 'Davy Bossin', I find that though my father was as discreet a man as ever broke the law, I can still pick up his trail seventy years later.

The earliest reference I have found is in the *Toronto Daily Star* of June 20, 1938. At that time, Davy was delivering instantaneous racing results and news to Toronto's leading bookmakers. This took him into in a legal grey area. There had been as yet no Canadian charged with abetting bookmaking by providing betting information over the phone. In the United States there had been a few cases, but they had ended in acquittals. This would soon change, sparked by the prosecution of Moses Annenberg.

But that was a year away when Doug McQuarrie, the *Star's* racing columnist, devoted his June 20 edition of 'Along Turf Row' to one of Davy's yarns. After his tips of the day—Toe Dance, Hey Kelly, and Surcharge in the first, Sisweep, Tabmark, Regalite in the second—he reported: 'Davy Bossin, out enjoying a bit of Toronto's night life, so called, tells a good one. It seems a bookie was getting considerable action from a certain chap. The fellow would come in before the first race and bet until he was blue in the face. But nothing ever happened for him. Day after day, race after race, he lost. And he bet pretty good too. There was apparently no limit to the money he could lose. One thing was definite—he never won.

'One day he became a little fed up. He'd been betting with the book for two weeks and hadn't cashed a bet. He'd blown in the neighbourhood of $2000. He went over to the bookie and declared he was through. It wasn't the money. It was betting on horses that never even received a call.

'The bookie was worried. After all, bookies don't pick up easy money like this every day in the week. The book told him his luck was bound to change and since he was given to betting long shots, when he did win, the horse would pay off at astounding odds—it was bound to be limits.

'So the bettor continued to bet. He picked them longer and crazier. As time wore on he became more disgusted than ever. Finally, he told the

book, "Give me $100 straight on so-and-so, and I swear, if he doesn't get a call, I quit. That's definite. No call, I'm through." The bookie hated to see his customer so unhappy, a man who was, after all, a source of very good action. So what's he to do? He knew the pelt the man bet on wasn't worth a quarter. But he had an idea.

'He gets on the phone and calls up the fellow who broadcasts the racing service to all the joints in town. "Look," the bookie tells the service man, "I've got a mark here who threatens to quit me if the next horse he wagers on doesn't get a call. You're the one person who can save me. Can you just mention the name of the horse once? Put him in at the quarter. That's all I ask."

'The race comes up. The service man opens the mike. The book is holding the mark's C-note on Big Chocolate. The nag hasn't a chance. Still, off in one corner, the heavy bettor has his ear cocked. "They're off an' running!" the service man tells his unseen audience. "At the quarter, it's Whozits by a length, its Whatzis by a half. Sure Pop is third, and fourth is … Big Chocolate."

'"There, ya see," the bookie shouts to his customer, "your horse got a call."

'Again the announcer's voice comes over the speaker. "They're at the half. It's Whozits by a half, Watzis is second by a head. Big Chocolate is third." The bookie is happy as a lark. Not only has the service man given Big Chocolate a call at the quarter, he had the skate up there at the half! Now that's a real pal.

'At the six-furlong mark another call comes through. "It's Whozits by a half, Watzis is still second by a head. Big Chocolate on the outside, is third, running handily." The bookie is laughing noticeably by this time. The customer is excited. He'd blown $2000 and never got a call. Now, just as he is about to quit, he picks a live one.

'As the field hits the stretch another call comes through. "It's Whozits by a head. It's Whatsis by a neck. Big Chocolate is third and closing ground." Boy oh boy, is he making this close, the bookie thinks. Both bookie and bettor have a picture of the race in their minds. The bookie sees his customer's choice running in the can. The call is a joke. The bettor sees his first get in a dog's age.

'The announcer breaks the silence. "At the wire … it's Big Chocolate by a nose! Whozits is second and Whatzis is third. And," he adds, as if specifically for the aghast bookie, "this call ain't no phoney!" The book

nearly has a fit. The horse really does pay limits. It costs the book $1500 dollars. But still, he's up $500 on the guy over two weeks, and he sees a bright future ahead, a very bright future indeed.'

MOSES ANNENBERG'S CASE went to the grand jury on June 7, 1939, and, not coincidentally, within a few days a man named George Laflamme hailed my father on the street. Laflamme told Davy he was starting up a handbook and wanted to subscribe to the race wire. As was his practice, Davy listened to Laflamme in silence. Then he told him he couldn't help him, but would mention his request to Mexican Pete, if he ran into Pete. Mexican Pete subsequently called Laflamme, who invited Pete over to his book. It was a bare attic room with a table and several telephones, a typical bookie's back end. Mexican Pete offered to deliver the racing news by phone to Laflamme for twelve dollars a week. Or so said James Crichton, who was listening in Laflamme's closet. Crichton and Laflamme, whose real name was John George Jenkins, were cops. They had been assigned to entrap my father into knowingly selling racing information to a book-maker, thereby clearly breaking a law that had proven slippery and difficult to enforce. The ruse was the first shot in a legal offensive that would culmi-nate, two months later, in Davy's arrest. The news would be splashed across the front pages of all the Toronto newspapers. Mercifully, my grandfather had not lived to see it.

Davy's vocation had always been anathema to his father. Zussman Bossin was a pillar of the Jewish community in the Ward, as he had been in Brusilov in the Old Country. 'Of course, Zussie was a great man,' one of my aunts told me once. To her it was a simple, obvious fact. Zussman was learned; he taught himself Hebrew, Yiddish, Russian and English; he wrote poetry; he helped his fellow immigrants negotiate the Canadian legal sys-tem; he was president of the *russische shul* and head of the *kashruth* author-ity, the board responsible for kosher foods; he was a man of integrity and, by hook or by crook, by belt or by hand, he instilled it in his children. Davy—Davy the Punk—got the worst of it.

Davy's line of work was all the more painful for Zussman, because Davy was his father's favourite. My grandfather saw Davy's genius early. 'My father had no use for school,' my aunt Celia remembered. 'As soon as we were old enough, we were expected to go to work. Morning after morning, when I was leaving the house, Zussie would say, "*Asa shteellina, shteinina, eisena! Nokhamol geht in schule? Ge arbiten!* You're a girl of steel,

stone and iron. Again you are going to school? Go to work!" But Davy—
that was a whole different story. For Davy, he would have done anything.
He wanted Davy to be a lawyer.'

Davy's only interest in the law, however, was how to get around it. To
him, Canadian law was as foreign and remote as rabbinical law. And he was
as tough and stubborn as his father. So Davy left home, with its quarrels
and beatings, when he was little more than a boy. Still, he and Zussman
never grew estranged. Every Friday night, Davy was back at the family
table for *shabbes* dinner.

For all the family conflict Davy's occupation stirred up, it was ulti-
mately his gambling income that raised the Bossins out of poverty. Through
the Depression years, Davy supported his parents and siblings. For
instance, he bought Chava, my grandmother, a refrigerator—the first in the
neighbourhood. As if by magic, it kept food cold without blocks of ice.
Davy's sisters, who still lived at home, moved the contents of the ice box to
the refrigerator. Chava watched skeptically. Sure enough, the seltzer stayed
cold. The refrigerator was an amazing invention and a wonderful gift. But
two days later Sady and Celia found the food back in the icebox. So once
again they explained to Chava how the new invention worked, and moved
the food to the refrigerator. A day later, it was back in the icebox.

With two sons who became newspaper columnists, the life of my
grandmother was well, if sentimentally, recorded. My uncle Hye dubbed
her 'America's Other Mother'. In a sense she was. She could have been the
poster girl for the great migration. She was diminutive in height, round in
shape, with glasses as thick as Coke bottles. She never learned to read or
write; she signed her name with an X. Chava's limited English was heavily
accented and she constantly reversed words. She would ask for a 'Cola-
Coca', or talk about the beautiful 'maidsbrides'. My aunt Celia would
explain to her that the English was 'bridesmaid'. 'The bride comes first, the
maid comes after,' she'd say, '*verstehen?*' Chava would nod and smile, and
Celia would say, 'Ma, let me hear you say it,' and Chava would say 'maids-
bride'. This would exasperate and amuse her children no end, which was
probably why Chava said it the way she did.

Chava's children were also amused and perplexed by her walking.
Chava loved to walk (perhaps to escape her endless family responsibilities).
She walked for miles, tirelessly, all over Toronto, including one winter's
night late in her life when there was a terrible storm. As she put on her coat
and galoshes, her daughters demanded to know why she insisted on going

Chava with my mother

out when it was snowing so hard she could hardly see. 'Nu, vos es is, vos ich vel nicht sein?' she replied, So what is there that I won't see?

The children of America's Other Mother loved to tell stories like that, of what they saw as Chava's innocence, leaving unacknowledged her strength and canniness. When Zussman, in righteous indignation, would lock the front door to keep Davy out of the house, Chava would unlock the back door. In later years, Davy—who never had a bank account— stored his money in a trunk under Chava's bed. The family story was that, in her naiveté, she did not know. But of course she did. For my grandmother, it was just one more of the strange ways of the *goldene medina*, where God landed her to raise her eleven children. That they survived and remained loyal to one another was her quiet triumph. In 1950, Davy, my mother and I were still going to my grandmother's on Friday nights for *shabbes* dinner.

Chava died on Victoria Day in 1952. My uncle Hye wrote in his column, 'The early life of such mothers was a constant struggle. Yet they needed only half a chance to have a good time. They mastered the life they were born into, but life seems to have mastered most of us, with prestige and money not being the help we imagined. And all the while, there was the example of *their* lives to teach us. The world, as the rabbi said, is poor in such mothers.'

I was six when Chava died. I remember the icebox that was still in use in her kitchen, and the plastic oxygen tent through which I last saw her. And I remember my father: it was the only time I ever saw Davy cry.

ZUSSMAN HAD DIED sixteen years before Chava, on Labour Day, 1936, at the age of seventy. That summer my grandparents had vacationed at a hot spring in Michigan. Because of his age, the attendants warned Zussman to forgo the hottest pool, but he brushed them off. He had a heart attack. He recovered, but then, with the arrival of autumn, he set about his usual preparations for winter, including shovelling out the coal cellar. There he had a second, and fatal, heart attack. His funeral was attended by hundreds. 'He must have been well liked,' I said to Aunt Celia.

'No,' she replied, 'he wasn't. But he was respected.'

No doubt. He was smart, tough, righteous and accomplished, all in the face of unremitting poverty and prejudice. But to me, the most remarkable thing about Zussman was his surprising flexibility, which ran like an underground stream beneath the rock of his will. After his battles with Davy, Zussman accepted that his children were going to be Canadians, and only incidentally Jews. He would continue his Old World religion and ways, they would find theirs. Years later, when his friends' sons and

Zussman

daughters were doctors and lawyers, Zussman belatedly acknowledged his own short-sightedness. '*Ich hob gehat brillanten, ober ich hob es nicht versteht*—I had diamonds,' he said, 'and I didn't know it.'

Eventually, Zussman even came to terms with the notoriety of his prodigal son, Davy. My aunt Sally, the last of Zussman's and Chava's children, told me that, one afternoon, she and her father were walking along Queen Street when an old man called out, '*Sholom aleychem*, Zussman.'

'*Aleychem sholom*,' Zussman answered in the traditional reply, but then recognizing the man, he added excitedly, '*Shmul? Es is du?*' The men embraced like the old friends they in fact were. They spoke animatedly in Yiddish. Zussman asked Shmul about his children, and he answered proudly that this one was a lawyer, this one a doctor, this one an accountant. 'And your boys?' he asked Zussman.

'*Gut*,' Zussman said. 'Art is making movies in Hollywood, Hye is a writer.'

'And Dovid?'

'Ah, Dovid.' Zussman paused a moment, stood straighter and informed his old friend, 'Dovid is an expert on horses.'

ON AUGUST 4, 1939, two months after 'George Laflamme' stopped Davy on the street, Constable Herb Thurston was ordered to report to the band room above the police garage on Dundas Street. He did not know it, but he was there to participate in the biggest raid Toronto's police had ever undertaken. The target was the *Canadian Racing and Financial News*.

When Thurston arrived at the garage, he joined nearly forty other policemen who had been similarly summoned with no explanation. Charlie Scott was making sure that this time there would be no leaks and no tip-offs. Staff Inspector Charlie Scott was one of Toronto's highest-ranking police officers, and the head of the anti-gambling squad. He was a burly, ruddy-complexioned Irishman, who had joined the force in 1910. He hated gamblers. Scott had personally overseen the arrest of over five hundred of them, and then watched them go right back at it a few days later. 'This time,' he told the assembled policemen, 'we are going to deal the bookies a death blow. We are going to smash their nerve centre. We are going to shut down the race wire permanently.'

The raiding party left the police garage and drove to Mercer Street. They surrounded the *Canadian Racing and Financial News* building. At 2:37 p.m., the command came over the brand-new police radio system. Thurston

charged in and ran up the stairs to the second floor, just in time to see Davy slip his arm under the wires plugged into his switchboard, and pull them all out at once. Charlie Scott ordered his men to 'rip everything out of there except the wallpaper.' This they did. They removed equipment, papers, furniture, and even the wiring under the floor. It took them all night and into the next day. They arrested Davy, Sam Roher, the telegrapher, the stenographer and the eighteen telephone girls. In another of several simultaneous raids they busted Mexican Pete, who had sold the racing news service to 'George Laflamme'.

The telephone girls were soon released without charge. (In fact, their actions were well within the law.) The men were released, each on $2,000 bail (over $30,000 today). R.H. Greer, K.C., appeared for Davy and his colleagues, and requested that the trial be scheduled as soon as possible, so that some forty people could return to work. Crown Attorney J.W. McFadden argued that it would take considerable time to prepare such a large and important case. Magistrate 'Honest Bob' Brown granted McFadden the time he needed. Meanwhile, Charlie Scott informed the press that the flow of illegal bets in Ontario had slowed to a trickle.

It took four months for McFadden and Scott to put together their case. They had tons of evidence—literally—and they assembled a dozen witnesses to testify. By December 1939, they were ready to throw the book at Davy and his colleagues. The case was straightforward. The problem was, the law was not. In fact, when it came to Davy's particular crime, the Criminal Code of Canada was virtually impenetrable.

The gambling sections of the Criminal Code reflected the ambivalence of Canadian society and of the parliamentarians who tried to square the circle. Under Section 202, bookmaking was illegal but betting was not. Too many senators owned racehorses for that. And since wagering on horses was legal, it could hardly be illegal to provide information to help people do so more prudently. In fact, racing tips and results were a mainstay of Canadian newspapers, accounting for a substantial chunk of their circulation. On the editorial page of the *Toronto Daily Star*, the paper's publisher 'Holy Joe' Atkinson might fulminate against the evils of gambling, but in a box on the bottom right-hand corner of the front page of the afternoon editions, the *Star* ran the latest race results in red ink.

So, under the Criminal Code, providing racing information was legitimate but from 1908 on, the law forbade anyone to '*willfully and knowingly* send, transmit, deliver or receive any message by radio, telegraph,

telephone, mail or express that conveys any information relating to book-making, pool-selling, betting or wagering, or that is *intended to assist in bookmaking*, pool-selling, betting or wagering' (my italics). Accordingly, race results reported in a newspaper for the edification of the public were legitimate; providing the same results to bookmakers was a crime.[1] For Scott and McFadden, the intent of the law was clear, but it was undercut by the weaselly adverbs 'willfully and knowingly'. Undoubtedly bookies read the racing information in the *Star* and used it for their illegal business, but the newspaper did not *willfully and knowingly* print the information primarily for bookmakers' eyes. Davy, on the other hand, knew who his customers were. But did he know they were bookies? That they were, and that Davy knew they were, was what the Crown had to demonstrate.

The case against the *Canadian Racing and Financial News* came to trial on December 13, 1939, and it ran for a week. Magistrate Robert Forsythe presided. In those days, some of Toronto's magistrates had legal backgrounds and others did not. Forsythe did, and was known as a stickler. His reputation was above reproach.

Most of the trial was taken up by the parade of witnesses and evidence presented by the Crown. McFadden opened his case by filling the courtroom with the switchboards, telephone consoles and telegraph equipment captured in the raid. Police and telephone-company witnesses explained how the equipment worked and how it was used by the *Canadian Racing and Financial News*. Charlie Scott explained how bookies depended on the information. He also reported that one of his officers had seen Davy pull the wires from his switchboard, preventing the police from tracing the numbers to which he had been connected. (In those pre-computer years, Bell Telephone kept no record of local calls.)

McFadden then called to the stand the Secretary of the Ontario Jockey Club, followed by the President of the Ontario Horse Breeders' Association. Both men testified that the content of the *Canadian Racing and Financial News* contained little information that was of interest to horsemen or breeders. McFadden asked them if they considered the Scratch Sheet a legitimate newspaper. They did not.

1 This distinction was a Canadian one. In the United States, there was no law against providing information that facilitated illegal betting until 1961 when Robert Kennedy belatedly outlawed the race wire. In Britain such a law is unthinkable.

Finally, Constable John George Jenkins was called. He recounted his career as George Laflamme, noting that the wire service Mexican Pete had supplied went dead at 2:39 p.m., August 4—the exact time Davy pulled the wires from his switchboard.

Summing up the Crown's case, McFadden argued that only one reasonable conclusion could be drawn from the overwhelming evidence: a subscription to the *Canadian Racing and Financial News* was nothing more than a dodge enabling bookies to purchase the race wire to abet them in their unlawful activity.

Davy and his colleagues were represented by two prominent Ontario barristers, D.L. McCarthy, K.C., and R.H. Greer, K.C. McCarthy and Greer called no witnesses. They simply argued that the news their clients provided was virtually the same as that published in the *Daily Racing Form* or, for that matter, in the *Toronto Daily Star*. Accordingly, they asked, should not the *Canadian Racing and Financial News* enjoy the same legal protections? It simply disseminated its news faster. The paper's telephone services were, according to McCarthy, a clever gimmick to increase subscriptions—in the best free-enterprise tradition. 'For the purpose of selling our paper, we have evolved this ingenious device,' McCarthy told the Court. 'I won't say that the odd person doesn't use it in making bets, but the Crown has to go further than that. They have to demonstrate evil intent; they have to demonstrate that we willfully and knowingly intended to assist in bookmaking; and about that, they have offered no evidence.'

When McCarthy had finished, Magistrate Forsythe needed no time to deliberate. 'My sympathies are entirely with the Crown,' he said. 'However, there is such a narrow margin of difference between the operations of the *Canadian Racing and Financial News* and those of other racing periodicals sanctioned in this country, that the demarcation is too thin for a conviction....

'The Crown has asked me to assume that no one would want to know the outcome of a horse race immediately after the race, unless he was interested in making or taking illegal bets. This assumption, I regret I am unable to make. I cannot convict upon a negative hypothesis. It would be a most dangerous precedent. I therefore, regretfully, discharge the accused men.'

The months of preparation, the ton of equipment hauled into the courtroom, and the days of testimony by the experts were, in the end, insufficient. The case had been lost when Davy greeted George Laflamme with his customary silence, foiling the effort to entrap him. It was lost again

when he pulled the wires from his switchboard, leaving at the centre of the Crown's case only a 'negative hypothesis' about who his customers were. Davy and his colleagues were free. Mexican Pete—whose real name was Harry Desenhouse—pleaded guilty to knowingly providing Constable Jenkins with the race wire. Pete was fined $200. The next day, he was back at work.

The Crown appealed, but the Court of Appeal refused to review the case, because the fastidious Magistrate Forsythe had made no error in law. Inspector Scott and Crown counsel McFadden were fit to be tied. What Davy was up to was plain as day; only a pedant like Forsythe could not see it. Still, Charlie Scott could comfort himself that he had shut down the nerve centre of Toronto bookmaking for the four months it took the case to come to trial. And that hiatus killed the *Canadian Racing and Financial News.* Alas for Scott, the bookies were a wily bunch and had quickly filled the void with other sources for the news they needed.

Two days after the verdict, an ad appeared in the *Globe and Mail* which read:

<div align="center">

Daily Turf and Sporting News.

Free Phone Service.

Sold at all news-stands.

25 cents.

</div>

I CAN ONLY REMEMBER my father ever telling two jokes, both about a character named Benny Bermuda. Truth to tell, Davy's jokes were more like fables. Jokes were simply not in Davy's nature. He was a realist, firmly rooted in the hardscrabble life of the street. For Davy, the streets of Toronto *were* paved with gold, and so filled with ironies that jokes were superfluous.

In any case, as Davy told it, Benny Bermuda was born on July 7, 1907, 'the seventh day of the seventh month of the seventh year. Seventy years later, on the eve of his seventieth birthday, Benny had a dream. He dreamed he was shooting craps. There were hundred-dollar bills scattered all over the table. And when it came Benny's turn to roll, he threw a seven. Just as he raked in his money, he awoke to the song of birds. There were seven song sparrows sitting on the wire outside Benny's window.

'Benny got up and drank his usual half-dozen cups of coffee, but then,

in the spirit of the day, he had a fateful seventh cup. And as he did, he opened the *Racing Form* and there, on page seven, he saw that the seventh horse in the seventh race at Hialeah was called Lucky Number Seven—7 to 1 on the morning line.

'Benny was not a superstitious man. Still, he dressed hastily and hurried to his bank. He withdrew seven thousand dollars. He stuffed the cash in his pocket and headed to his bookie's, where he put the whole seven thousand on the nose of Lucky Number Seven.

'And damned if Lucky Number Seven didn't come in.

'Seventh.'

• • • 11. Marci • • •

THE RAID on the *Canadian Racing and Financial News* on August 4, 1939, took place a few months after my father and mother married. Yet when I asked my mother about it, she said it never happened. When I told her I had dug up the news coverage, she said she had no recollection of it, and it must not have been a big deal. (It was front page news in all the Toronto papers.) 'Your father never went to jail,' she added.

That conversation took place some forty-five years after the fact, which could have contributed to my mother's forgetfulness. I also suspect that, like most men in those days, Davy did not share business details with his wife. And I would bet that he assured her the bust was a nuisance and nothing more. But still—a new bride, her husband arrested, front-page stories. You would think she would remember. Perhaps she did, but preferred not to say so. My mother's silence could be as profound as my father's, but where he clammed up, she surrounded her secrets in an impenetrable thicket of misdirection.

My mother, Marci Bossin, was a character. She was elegant, popular and glamorous. 'She was the most beautiful woman in Toronto,' the former maitre d' of the Club Indigo told me. 'She had the most gorgeous eyes you

ever saw,' said Gerri Washkov, an old family friend, 'pansy-coloured eyes. You think Elizabeth Taylor had the eyes! Marci had them first.'

With Marci, beauty was not just skin deep. 'I loved anything that was beautiful,' she told me, at eighty-something. 'Beautiful music. People who were beautiful. Beauty just turned me on.' She drew, sculpted, and painted all her life and became an accomplished and recognized artist at a time when few women did. 'Nothing was as satisfying as painting,' she told me. 'Other than a good lover.'

When she wanted to be, Marci was like that, disarmingly candid. When push came to shove, she was street-wise, clear-headed, succinct. But when push did *not* come to shove, in the normal round of conversation, my mother took on the protective colouring of Mrs Malaprop or Gracie Allen. The form was funny and convivial, the content irretrievable. People loved it. I hated it.

I once asked my 'Aunt' Gerri Washkov about Marci's dizzy façade. Gerri was one of those honorary aunts. She was a gravel-voiced, shoot-from-the-hip old radical and veteran of the Yiddish theatre. I loved her from as far back as I can remember. Late in her life, I visited her in her retirement home, and as the conversation drew to a close, I gingerly raised the subject of Marci's persona, and my discomfort with it. 'My mom has this way of speaking,' I ventured hesitantly, 'that is, you know ... um ... sort of ...'

'Ditzy,' Gerri said.

'Exactly,' I said, delighted to hear, after so many years, that I wasn't the only one who noticed. 'Was she always ... so ..?'

'Ditzy?' she said. 'Always.'

'But,' she went on, 'you have to understand what it was like back then. Most apartments wouldn't rent to Jews. Resorts had signs that said "Restricted Patronage". There used to be a sign on the Lakeshore as you drove into town that said "No dogs or Jews allowed". Somebody took it to court, but the sign was on private property and the judge upheld the owner's right to free speech.

'You lived with it every day. I'll never forget, I was looking for a job—I couldn't have been more than sixteen—and I saw an ad for work in a glove factory. I rushed to the building, went up several floors and found the door. PHILLIPS GLOVE COMPANY was painted on the glass. I went in and they took me to Mr Phillips. He hired me on the spot and said, "You can start on Monday." But he kept looking at me. He walked me back to the door, and finally he said, "And tell me, what church does your family

Marci c. 1928

attend?" I said, "We don't go to church, we go to synagogue." He opened
the door for me and then said "Oh, you know what? I have your address,
don't come Monday, I'll contact you about when to come in."

'"You know damn well you won't!" I said. I slammed the door and the
glass pane with PHILLIPS GLOVE COMPANY on it shattered into a hun-
dred pieces.

'That was the way it was. And if you were not only a Jew but a woman,
you had two strikes against you. You had to develop some way of coping,
or you would go crazy. For me, it was the theatre, the politics. You did
whatever worked. For Marci it was being ditzy.'

MY MOTHER WAS BORN in 1912, née Marcella Louise Levitt. Her
father, A.J., was a successful furrier, who had come to Toronto from
Poland via New York. Her mother, Selma, was a ramrod-straight Toronto
bourgeoise, who had left behind her Polish-immigrant, garment-factory life
when she married A.J.

Selma sent her only daughter—my mother had four brothers—to the
exclusive Normal Model School. She drilled Marci on manners and

deportment. A.J., on the other hand, delighted in his daughter's high spirits and creativity. Marci studied dance and performed at Massey Hall in a company that then moved on to New York, where they joined the Rockettes at Radio City Music Hall. But Selma put her foot down, and Marci stayed in Toronto. Marci also sang. As a child, she was taken to sing for the cantor, a stern man in black gabardine with a long black beard. The audition was in someone's kitchen where, amid the clatter of the supper preparations, the man commanded Marci to sing 'God Save the King'. She stammered a few lines. He stopped her and pronounced, 'This child will never sing.'

Marci switched to painting. With A.J.'s encouragement, she planned to go to New York to study clothing design when she was old enough. When she was sixteen her portfolio won her early acceptance to the Ontario College of Art, and A.J. convinced Selma that Marci should leave high school for art college. The Group of Seven were Marci's teachers. Franz Johnston was a particular mentor. She recalled her first encounter with him, 'I found an easel and watched as the model entered, walked to the dais and threw off her robe. I was so embarrassed that I spent the entire class working with my back to her. Finally, Mr Johnston came by and said, "Mees Levitt, if you do not wish to observe zee model, zat is your choice. But you must know, zey are hround, not sqvare!"'

A.J. died suddenly in 1928, from appendicitis. Marci's dream of designing clothing died with A.J. For Selma, it was too close to the *shmata* trade she had risen above. She pulled Marci out of the College of Art and enrolled her in secretarial school.

Through family connections, Marci found a job at Simpson's Department store. Unlike Eaton's, the Robert Simpson Company hired Jews for its store, although they liked to keep Jewish employees off the sales floor. Somehow this was overlooked with Marci (who did not look Jewish) and she was assigned to the fur department. With her beauty, her good manners from Selma, and her knowledge of furs from A.J., she excelled and continued to work on the floor. One day a woman approached her, pointed to a dark-complexioned saleswoman and said to Marci, 'Will you help me? I don't want to be served by that Jewish girl.' The other salesgirl was not, in fact, Jewish. Marci, who was, got the sale.

Eventually Marci was given the job of designing the displays for the store's show-room windows along Queen Street.

My mother always spoke of her girlhood as sheltered, stifled by

Selma's Victorian pretensions and demands. She remembered the time her mother 'cleaned up' her studio while she was out, tossing the sculptures she was working on into the garbage. She remembered the way Selma would stand behind the backs of the young men who came to take her out. Selma would shake her head and make a disdainful face to signal, 'He is not good enough for you.'

'Even in the 1960s, when I was having shows and selling my paintings,' Marci recalled, 'Mother would phone and say "What are you doing?" If I told her I was painting, she would get very annoyed. After awhile, I got smart and I'd tell her I was doing housework. She'd say, "That's a good girl!"'

Selma's training was, however, only marginally successful. Marci always had a Bohemian side. As a young woman, she would camp on the Humber River with the art school crowd. She smoked. By the latter 1930s, when Marci was in her late twenties and still unmarried, she and some girlfriends took a summer apartment at Hanlan's Point, a down-at-heel community on one of the islands in Lake Ontario, just south of Toronto. When Selma would come to visit, someone would run ahead from the ferry to warn Marci and her roommates to clean up and send off the young men who were a constant presence in the apartment.

Marci's flat was on the ground floor. Upstairs was another apartment, which, as fate would have it, Davy had rented for himself and his brother Hye. Hye Bossin was a ladies' man, handsome—he was the spitting image of the movie star Pat O'Brien—athletic, witty and outgoing. Davy, who by then was in his thirties, was quiet and reserved. He was considered a confirmed bachelor. Hye would often entertain a date in the brothers' apartment, and Davy would, helpfully, visit downstairs, sleeping over when Hye's date lasted all night. On those nights, and other social occasions, he always seemed to wind up next to Marci. They began to court in earnest. Davy would return late from the city by rowboat, after the last ferry to Hanlan's Point had sailed. He would pick up Marci and row her through the lagoons while she sang to him. Surprisingly, Selma approved of Davy. Marci and Davy married on a Saturday morning in May of 1939. He was thirty-four, she was twenty-seven. At my father's insistence, it was a simple city hall ceremony, with only their mothers in attendance. Then he went back to work, announcing the day's races. Marci joined her friends in a baseball game.

Marci and Davy had no honeymoon until the following winter when

they spent several weeks at Ste-Agathe, Quebec, courtesy of a colleague of Davy's who needed him out of town so he could not be subpoenaed. They stayed in a cabin at the foot of the ski hill and entertained a stream of visitors, Davy's gambling-business colleagues out from Montreal.[1]

As Marci's honeymoon went, so went the marriage. Davy went his own way, to his own drummer. Money was not a problem. They lived simply, as he preferred, and comfortably. Occasionally Marci would accompany Davy on a trip to one or another of the great 'carpet joints'—combined luxury restaurants, night clubs and gambling halls—of eastern America. But mostly she kept house, taught herself to cook, entertained herself and developed her painting. Though they stayed together for twenty-four years, until Davy's death, it was not an easy marriage for Marci. 'Your father really was a bachelor at heart,' my mother told me. 'He was a good man, don't get me wrong. He didn't drink, he didn't gamble, he didn't run around.' He also didn't want children. Marci did, and had assumed they would have a family. 'I guess we had never talked about it. You didn't in those days. Or I was just naive.' Davy, however, was adamant. 'Over my dead body,' he told Marci. 'If you want a baby, you will have to find another husband.'

AFTER THEIR ACQUITTAL in December 1939, Sam Roher, the official owner of the *Canadian Racing and Financial News*, and Davy, its manager, decided to separate the components of the business. The printing of the Scratch Sheet and the call-in service, where 'telephone girls' gave out coded race results, started up again in the old quarters on Mercer Street. In

1 One of the visitors was the Montreal gambling kingpin, Max Shapiro, who wanted to talk to Davy about an idea he had, a legitimate business to launder some of his income. Shapiro wanted to build, in Montreal, the most luxurious Chinese restaurant in the country. He invited Davy to be a partner. Davy declined. My father did, however, provide the restaurant with its kitchen staff, by hiring away the chefs from the excellent but dingy 'Number Seven' restaurant in Toronto's Chinatown. Ruby Foo's opened in 1945. It was a runaway success and became a Montreal landmark. When Max Shapiro's twin sons, Bernard and Harold, graduated from McGill, he hired them to manage the business. Eventually, the Shapiro boys returned to university. Bernard would become Principal of McGill and then Canada's Ethics Commissioner. Harold became President of Princeton.

Gordon Sinclair

the hair-splitting world of Canada's gambling laws, these services were legal. What my father did was not legal, if only it could be proved. Proof, however, was of marginal consequence; legal or not, Davy's operation remained fixed in the lawmen's cross-hairs. So Roher and my father moved Davy's phone service to its own premises, where further raids would not disrupt the Scratch Sheet's other functions.

They were wise to do so. The morality squad commenced a series of harassing raids, culminating in one that was reported as it occurred on April 25, 1940, by Gordon Sinclair, then a reporter for the *Toronto Daily Star*. The headline read, 'Crash! Bang! Come Echoes Of Race Wire Raid Over 'Phone.' Sinclair's article began:

'Hey, listen, I'm being raided. By cops. I'm being raided by cops right this very minute.' This frantic announcement came over the telephone to the *Star* office this afternoon and a mildly disbelieving reporter asked, 'What joint is being raided?'

'My joint. I'm the *Canadian Turf and Sports Bulletin* ... and they are knocking my place apart with sledge hammers. Do you hear that?' The reporter heard noises as though someone was building a boat.

'I'll call you back,' the reporter said, a standard precaution.... Then we called back and it took a long time to get an answer.... [Eventually we] got this answering reward.

'Hey, call back some other time, will ya. The cops is here and they're giving us the business.'

'Giving who the business?'

'Listen Mister, we got no time for answering riddles. The law is on us. The law, see, and they are taking the walls down.'

'Well, who is the manager? He called us.'

There was a loud boom as though somebody had just exploded a mine; then from off-stage, we heard a voice saying, 'Put that back. Put that back, I tell ya!'

Finally Davy picked up the phone:

'This is Dave,' he said.

'Gord Sinclair,' I said.

'Well, come on over here,' manager Dave Bossin said. 'This is a raid. Just one more raid and it has gone beyond any stage except persecution. They have raided each and every day for ten days. They never say why they come, never show a warrant and never make a pinch. They just break in, sledge around with hammers and

clubs and walk out again. This time they say they are making a pinch and I'm the pinch, which is dandy because now we'll get a chance to bring this thing before a court.'

At that point, Sinclair reported, the conversation broke off again and he heard scuffling, hammering and then:

'What's it to you who I'm talking to … I don't have to tell you, but since you are keen to know, it's the *Star*.'

Then Bossin came back on the wire to carry on the play-by-play description of the raid on his joint.

'Know what they are doing now? They are putting some of the furniture back. Yeah, they are trying to make out nothing happened. They got me talking to myself. Sledge hammers they bring, and now it's just a social visit or something. You better come right over here. Bring a camera. If you see someone lying on the ground it will be me.'

Later in the day, Sinclair interviewed Inspector Charlie Scott, who denied Davy's accusation. He told Sinclair:

'Police raiding squads are equipped with small sledge hammers which they carry up their sleeves. Today's raiders were so equipped but while they displayed the hammers on entering, they made no use of them and laid them on the table.

'Instead of raiding individual bookmakers, we now stage sit-arounds in clearing houses, where bookies phone to get results, approximate odds, prices and other information vital to the business. So far the system has been remarkably effective.'

Scott, like all police spokesman, was not one to downplay the success of his squad's operations, so his assessment has to be taken with a grain of salt. No matter. Whatever effect the 'sit-arounds' had, it was short-lived. Faced with ongoing harassment, Davy moved his operation to Forest Hill, a Toronto suburb which, at the time, had its own police force. The Forest Hill police, however, continued the nuisance raids, so that spring Davy bought a bungalow at 16 Royal York Road in faraway Etobicoke, on the western edge of Toronto. The Etobicoke police force consisted of two men, who had a reputation for being approachable. By summer, the *Weekly Sportsman*, as it had been renamed, was once again operating with impunity.

The biggest raid in Toronto's history and the harassment that followed had succeeded in driving Davy out of town, but not out of business.

OVER ALL, THE 1930s had been a long, disappointing decade for the opponents of gambling. Efforts to enforce the law had proven quixotic. But still the resolve of men like Charlie Scott held fast. Fortunately for them, as the 1940s unfolded, their campaign to vanquish the bookies would be reinvigorated by a fresh wave of anti-gambling fervour which once again swept north across the U.S. border. It had been Roosevelt's vendetta against Moses Annenberg that first cast the spotlight on Davy, sitting at his switchboard in his small corner of the racing business. By 1942, there was a new and compelling reason for shutting him down: the Mafia.

• • • 12. Costello • • •

MY FAVOURITE STORY about Frank Costello, the 'Prime Minister of the Underworld', was told to me by my cousin Benny Bossin, who is twenty years my senior. Benny and another cousin, Tevye Bossin, both married in June 1947. Their weddings were two days apart. For their honeymoons, the couples decided to travel together to New York City to see Joe DiMaggio and the Yankees play Hank Greenberg and the Detroit Tigers. DiMaggio was the biggest star since Babe Ruth, and Hank Greenberg was the hero of every Jewish boy. Tevye's father-in-law loaned them his car for the trip.

'Believe me, this was a big deal for four young, just-married kids,' Benny told me. 'I was still in university and Tev was an apprentice plumber. We were as poor as church mice, and about as naive. We figured we would just walk up to Yankee Stadium and pick up seats in the bleachers. That's how much we knew.

Frank Costello

'Your uncle Hye set us straight, and told us to try calling Davy—if anyone could get tickets, he could. I was a little reluctant. Your father was not a friendly guy and we all knew he had some shady connections. But I called him. He was pretty brusque but, in the end, he said he would fix us up, and told me to call him when we got to New York.

'It took us a whole day to drive. We were too broke to stop anywhere and rent rooms for an extra night, so we drove straight through. We finally reached Manhattan and checked into some dumpy hotel with Murphy beds. In the morning I phoned Davy. He gave me a number to call—no name, just a number. "Tell them I told you to call," he said.

'So I phoned and some guy answered, "Yeah." Nothing else, just "Yeah." I told him who I was, and he said, "Wait." Finally another voice came on, sort of a rough, hoarse whisper. He said there were tickets at the stadium in our name, and that we didn't have to pay, it was taken care of. We weren't expecting that. I said, "That's terrific" or something like that, and then he said, "You're the honeymooners, right?" I told him we were, and he asked what we planned to do after the game. As if we had plans. He said, "You wanna go to the Copacabana?" I said, thanks but we were on a pretty tight budget. He said, "Kid, don't worry about it. Just tell 'em you're Mr Bossin. You don't pay for nuttin'. But tip good. Then after the show, you can go over to the Latin Quarter for the second show."

'"Dress nice," he said, and hung up.

'That afternoon, we took the subway to Yankee Stadium and picked up our tickets. They were in the fourth row, right above third base, right behind where the President sits for the World Series. Hank Greenberg hit a home run.

'Then, that night, we got to the Copacabana, and I told them our name, and it's "Just a minute, Mr Bossin," and, so help me, they carried in a table and, just like in the movies, they put it down right in front of the front row, and that's where we sat. The chorus line practically kicked us. Sophie Tucker sang right in front of us.

'Well, a few years go by, and one day I'm watching the Kefauver hearings on television. Everybody watched them, it was the biggest thing on TV. The senators were grilling all these gangsters and crooked politicians, and suddenly I hear this voice I recognize. It's the same hoarse whisper I heard on the phone. I called Tev right away. "Turn on the TV!" I said. "It's the guy I talked to, the guy who got us the Yankees tickets. You know who those seats belonged to?"

'"Who?" he says.

'"Frank Costello, that's who."'

FRANK COSTELLO was born Francesco Castiglia in 1891 in the village of Lauropoli, in the arid Calabrian mountains of southern Italy. The village had been founded in the eighteenth century by an enlightened noblewoman, Marchesa Laura Serra, for whom it was named. The Marchesa populated Lauropoli by recruiting 'anyone who has trouble with justice, or is wanted by the law,' promising them and their families 'a nice house, work and full protection.'

Frank Costello's father, Don Luigi Castiglia, was not a criminal. He had been a soldier under Garibaldi and moved to Lauropoli in the 1870s, buying a farm with his army pension. But the farming was poor, too poor to support the large Castiglia family. In 1894, Don Luigi left for America. Francesco and his mother followed two years later.

Like the Ward in Toronto, to which the Bossins immigrated, or the Patch in Chicago where Moses Annenberg grew up, East Harlem was a far cry from the Castiglia family's hopes for America. The only jobs Don Luigi could find were as a labourer. The work was poorly paid and back-breaking. His wife ran a small grocery, working morning until night. Young Francesco stole of necessity. From the age of fourteen, he had scrapes with the law. Each time he was pinched, he gave the police a different name, in order to hide his previous arrests. Eventually he settled on the Irish-sounding alias, Frank Costello. In those years, the New York Police Department was Irish through and through. The Irish-dominated Tammany Hall ran New York City politics, dispensing jobs and patronage in return for the immigrants' votes. As an alias, Frank Costello seemed a smart choice.

Francesco knew this from experience. Once he had been caught red-handed, looting a vending machine. But just as the cop collared him, the local Tammany boss happened by. The Irish cop and the Irish ward heeler shared a joke and a wink, and then the Tammany man told the cop, 'I'll take care of this one.' The cop shrugged and walked away. 'I've just done you a favour,' the ward boss told Costello. 'Remember that, when I need a favour.' Costello remembered it all his life.

Costello's history of arrests eventually caught up to him. In 1915, when he was twenty-three, he was caught carrying a gun. The judge looked over his record and sentenced him to a year in prison. It was while serving

that sentence that he had a life-changing insight. 'I realized I was stupid,' he would tell his lawyer, friend, and biographer, George Wolf. 'Carrying a gun was like carrying a label that says, "I'm dangerous, I'm a criminal, get me off the streets." I made up my mind I would never pack a gun again, and I never did.' Costello decided his future lay in a more white-collar approach to crime. After his release from prison, he joined with a Jewish manufacturer of kewpie dolls and other novelty items. They manufactured punch boards, a popular form of saloon gambling of the day. The business prospered. Frank also worked as a bookie. Along with Meyer Lansky and Frank Erickson, he was taken under Arnold Rothstein's wing and schooled in the gambling business. Rothstein said he liked these boys because they were both smart and hungry. Then, in January 1920, Prohibition came into effect.

Crime is, on the whole, a young man's game. Al Capone, for instance, was twenty-nine at the peak of his career. By the time they reach their thirties, most wild young gangsters get married, settle down, and go more or less straight. But Prohibition interrupted the normal cycle. It was an offer too good for Frank Costello's generation to refuse. By banning supplies of liquor without dampening the demand for it, the American Volstead Act and its Canadian provincial counterparts offered the greatest affirmative action program for criminals ever devised. Costello and Capone, Lucky Luciano, Bugsy Siegel, Meyer Lansky and other young hoodlums found themselves with a gushing oil well on their turf. This generation of street punks could not settle down as they reached their thirties; they had too much money and too many responsibilities.

Prohibition raised crime to a level of profitability and a level of public acceptance that law-breaking had never before enjoyed, and no one profited more than Frank Costello. Blessed with a facility for organization, a gift for diplomacy, a visceral understanding of the efficacy of graft, and the mentorship of Arnold Rothstein, Costello came to run an enormous, multi-faceted industry.

Frank and his partners imported liquor from Europe to the island of Miquelon off southern Newfoundland; from there, they leased ships to carry it down the coast of the United States. At the limit of American territorial waters, the ships were met by an armada of speed-boats. The small but high-powered launches ran the liquor ashore, darting into obscure coves and bays. Costello even leased planes for reconnaissance and air cover. Once the contraband was ashore, a fleet of trucks moved it to

warehouses, where the liquor was watered down and then distributed to thousands of speakeasies.

To run such an extensive operation, Costello needed a reliable management team and an equally reliable paramilitary. So he recruited old friends and accomplices, among them Lansky, Siegel and the Mafia chieftain, 'Joe the Boss' Masseria. For capital, he partnered with financiers, some from the underworld, like Rothstein, and some from old, legitimate wealth, like Joseph Kennedy, the father of John F. Kennedy. (The Kennedy family has always denied the connection to Costello.) Finally, to keep things running smoothly, Costello developed a wide-ranging network of bribery and graft. Everyone was on Costello's pad, from judges, politicians and public officials down to members of the coast guard and cops on the beat. It was not unusual for the police to stand guard while shipments of liquor were unloaded. Sometimes they even pitched in and carried cases of booze themselves.

For a dozen years, the bootleggers and those they paid off profited handsomely. But with repeal in sight in the early 1930s, Costello and his colleagues knew they had to diversify. While some slipped into (or further into) prostitution, drugs, extortion, or labour racketeering, Costello, Lansky and other top bootleggers favoured the gambling business. The shift from the speakeasy to the carpet joint (and the numbers racket, the slots and the layoff business) was an easy one. Gambling lay somewhere between legitimate business and the other, rougher, rackets. The return on investment was as good or better, public acceptance greater, the legal penalties less onerous, and the *modus operandi* less violent. If a gambler or a bookie was slow to cover his losses, he rarely needed to be beaten up; refusing to take his bets (or his layoff money) was almost always enough to straighten him out. For the most part, the new boss gamblers left their baseball bats and brass knuckles on the streets of their youth, and adopted the demeanour and management style of the businessmen they had become. (Some, like Bugsy Siegel and Vito Genovese, continued to rely on violence. But even then, as Siegel once said, 'We only kill each other.')

The gambling business was a natural for Costello who drew on his association with Rothstein. Like A.R., Costello was an inveterate gambler. When Rothstein was murdered in 1928, Costello joined Frank Erickson to take over A.R.'s layoff business which, as described earlier, they then expanded into a coast-to-coast network. Davy ran the Toronto branch.

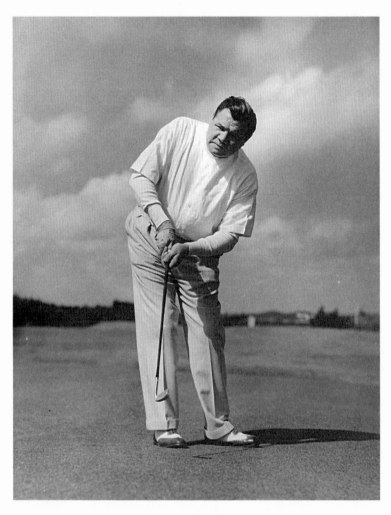

Babe Ruth

I BELIEVE FRANK COSTELLO and my father were friends as well as colleagues, though Davy never mentioned it, and if my mother knew anything, she didn't say. A few of Davy's friends, however, told me stories about Davy and 'Uncle Frank'. One recalled Costello dropping in on Davy at his booking agency in the Barclay Hotel in the 1950s. The two of them retreated to Davy's inner office and closed the door. I asked how he knew it was Costello. He laughed.

Another of Davy's pals remembered one particular story Davy told about Costello, because it involved Babe Ruth. Sometime in the late 1940s, Davy was in New York and had an appointment to meet Costello for dinner. Costello arrived late and explained that he had been golfing with the great Yankee home-run hitter. Ruth had retired from baseball, but was still a first-rate golfer. He was also a wastrel. Despite his wealth and fame, the 'Bambino', as he was aptly nicknamed, was frequently broke and would borrow money from his friends. Costello was happy to indulge Babe Ruth, but Ruth tended to forget to repay. Costello forgave this peccadillo, but the welching embarrassed him.

On this day, Ruth had once again asked Costello for a loan, this time $3000. Costello preferred to simply give him the money, so he conceived a clever pretext: he offered to bet $3000 on the next hole. Ruth, by far the better golfer, readily agreed, but to the great surprise of both men, Costello proceeded to hit a long, straight drive, and then a second shot that was equally, unusually precise. Costello's ball landed a few feet from the cup. He had never made an 'eagle' in his life, and now he had the opportunity to do so for the first time. But if he did, he would win the bet that he had cleverly set up to lose. In the end, Costello could not resist the eagle. He wound up loaning Ruth $6,000—the $3,000 he had asked for, and another $3,000 to cover the bet. Costello told Davy he knew he would never see the money again, but what could he do?

THE 1930S WERE THE GOLDEN AGE of the boss gamblers. Even when there was a burst of reform in one jurisdiction, the racketeers would be welcomed in the next with open arms (and outstretched hands). When the Republican reformer Fiorello LaGuardia was elected mayor of New York City in 1934, the operators simply slipped across the bridge to New Jersey. When LaGuardia took a sledgehammer to Costello's slot machines, Louisiana Governor Huey Long invited his friend Frank to move the business to New Orleans.

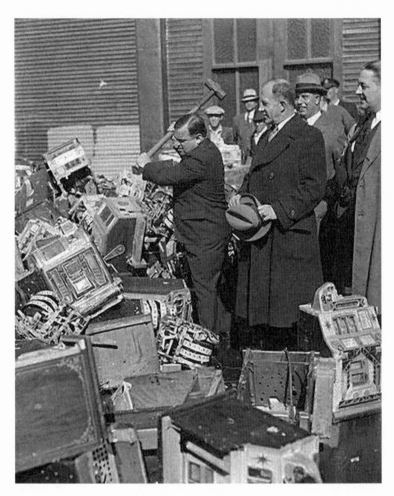

Fiorello LaGuardia, left

As the racketeers' operations expanded and spread, the need for more co-ordination among them grew. In 1929, at the President Hotel in Atlantic City, the top racketeers held their first 'convention'. It was chaired by Frank Costello. Following Costello's lead, the Mob bosses began to cooperate with each other more, and murder each other less. For his efforts, his colleagues nicknamed Costello 'the Prime Minister'. It was not entirely a compliment.

Costello, meanwhile, tightened the diplomatic ties between the underworld and official America, building on the empire Arnold Rothstein had left behind when he was shot in 1928. Costello became one of the most powerful figures in Tammany Hall, and thereby in New York politics. It was said that no judge could reach the bench in the state without Costello's approval. Frank's support for Franklin Roosevelt, whom he admired, helped Roosevelt win the Democratic nomination for President in 1932. The President and the 'Prime Minister' are known to have met on at least one occasion.

REMARKABLY, BEFORE 1951 few had heard of the Mafia. That would soon change, and the Mob would become one of the indelible icons of popular culture. Once it did, the myth quickly outstripped the reality. The Mafia has never been the omnivorous, international crime empire beloved of novelists, moviemakers and politicians. Of course there were, and are, Italian gangs, some of which have wielded considerable power and exacted considerable tribute. But they have never had the unanimity, reach, or diabolical clout of the fictional Sopranos or Corleones—Frank Costello's unifying efforts not withstanding.

Initially, the consolidation of organized crime, such as it was, went unnoticed by the authorities, though occasional prophetic voices warned of a growing, interconnected criminal network. Mostly, the top lawmen, including the FBI director, J. Edgar Hoover, dismissed the idea. Several of Hoover's biographers speculate that his reluctance to bell the cat was because he was, de facto, blackmailed: the mobsters had evidence that Hoover and Clyde Tolson, the FBI's deputy director, were lovers. The blackmail story and Hoover's sexual orientation remain unconfirmed, but there is no doubt that there was a détente of some sort between Hoover and Costello, who fed the FBI director tips on fixed horse races. Walter Winchell, the famous Broadway columnist, acted as the go-between. Costello liked to complain that it cost him thousands of dollars to buy a

race so Hoover could place a $10 bet. (In fact, while Hoover was at one window betting his $10, Tolson was at another, betting hundreds of dollars based on Costello's tips.)

Well into the 1940s, the FBI showed little interest in the Mafia. Hoover defended the Bureau's inaction by saying it had 'much more important functions' than arresting bookies. Many other lawmen offered the same justification. During Montreal's Caron Inquiry in the early 1950s, Judge Caron asked one police captain why he had so rarely collared gamblers or prostitutes. 'I was too busy arresting Communists,' he answered.

Eventually, however, the Mafia's free ride came to an end. Over the 1940s, the scattered voices decrying the advance of organized crime swelled to a mass chorus, a chorus conducted by the director of the Chicago Crime Commission, Virgil T. Peterson.

The Chicago Crime Commission (CCC) is a citizens' law-and-order lobby that continues to this day. It was first formed by wealthy businessmen in 1919, in the corrupt and violent Chicago of the Mont Tennes era. Impatient with the police force's unwillingness to act and the ineffectiveness of the courts, the CCC took it upon itself to protect the citizens and, in particular, the businesses of the city. They exposed Chicago's violence and corruption, feeding scoops (and unsupported accusations) to the press. It was the CCC that first published a Public Enemies list, with Al Capone at the top. The FBI stole the idea from the CCC.

Virgil Peterson took the helm of the Chicago Crime Commission in 1942, leaving a senior post with the FBI. (He had been second-in-command to the hotshot G-man Melvin Purvis back in the Bureau's heyday of gunning down bank robbers like John Dillinger, Pretty Boy Floyd and Baby Face Nelson.) In his new job, Peterson salted the country with crime commissions, creating a national vigilante movement. Whenever his crusade came up against reluctant officials—up to and including President Harry Truman, who was also on friendly terms with Costello—Peterson outflanked them by courting local governments and the press. Tirelessly, Peterson warned Americans (and, on his visits to Canada, Canadians) of the 'barbarians in our midst'. By the end of the decade, he had shamed even the mightiest skeptics, including Truman and Hoover, into joining his crusade.

By 1950, the public outcry orchestrated by Peterson made a full U.S. Senate investigation of organized crime inevitable. The chairmanship of the United States Special Committee to Investigate Crime in Interstate Commerce was given to Estes Kefauver, the junior Democratic Senator

from Tennessee. Kefauver was a senatorial nonentity at the time, and may have won the plum, high-profile position over fellow candidate Republican Senator Joseph McCarthy because the ruling Democrats believed that Kefauver was less likely to disturb the skeletons in Democratic closets. Though McCarthy failed to win the chairmanship of the crime committee, he was back a year later chairing the congressional hearings into Communist infiltration of government. McCarthy's name would become synonymous with congressional witch-hunts and guilt by accusation, but it was Kefauver who blazed the trail.

Like the trial in *Alice in Wonderland*, the Kefauver hearings started with the verdict: there existed a ubiquitous, centrally controlled, secret organization called the Mafia, which was responsible for most of the serious crime in America. Having settled that, the Committee called witnesses whose testimony provided the evidence. Kefauver had no time for criminologists, sociologists or other eggheads. Instead, the Committee travelled across the United States (skipping the home states of the committee members) interviewing crime commission spokesmen, chief prosecutors, and police chiefs.[1] They subpoenaed gangsters, suspect politicians and corrupt public officials. They even questioned the woman the papers called 'America's top moll', Virginia Hill.

The Kefauver hearings climaxed in New York with the testimony of the Committee's star witness, the man Kefauver and the press called 'the Prime Minister of the Underworld,' Frank Costello. Costello's original nickname, 'the Prime Minister' had been bestowed, with some irony, by his Mafia colleagues, but the irony was lost on the politicians, the press and, after the hearings, the American people, who followed every minute of Costello's interrogation by the senators on the new medium of television.

Midway though the Kefauver Committee's travels, a local television station in New Orleans requested and was granted permission to broadcast

1 In a glaring omission, Kefauver cancelled the Committee's scheduled public hearings in Chicago. Years later, Seymour Hersh reported in the *New York Times* that Chicago mobsters had arranged for Senator Kefauver to meet an attractive admirer in the bar of the stately Drake Hotel, where he was staying. The senator accompanied her to her room, which had been outfitted with a hidden infrared camera. When presented with photographs of his tryst, and a threat to release the pictures if the Chicago hearings went ahead, Kefauver cancelled the sessions.

Estes Kefauver

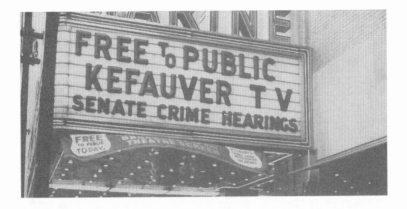

the Louisiana sessions. The result was electrifying. Television was just becoming popular and the TV audience was riveted by the 'facts' about graft, corruption and crime. Thousands tuned in to see the until-then shadowy underworld figures squirm under the senators' interrogation. After that, wherever the Committee went, its public sessions were televised. The audience numbered in the millions. The hearings drew more viewers than the 1951 World Series.

No effective legislation came out of the Kefauver Inquiry, yet it profoundly changed North American politics. The public's reaction to the Committee's revelations was as fervent as it was misinformed. The era of politics by television was underway.

IN THE BACK of every used bookstore you will find a shelf or two labelled 'True Crime', and eventually most of the books about organized crime turn up there. Like the Kefauver Committee's revelations, the paperbacks tend to be long on sensation and short on insight. But occasionally there is a book like *Little Man: Meyer Lansky and the Gangster Life*, by the British author Robert Lacey. Lacey's 1991 biography of Meyer Lansky is a rare treat: at nearly 700 pages, it is thoroughly researched, fully documented and elegantly written. But for me, *Little Man* offered an additional, personal epiphany, for it included an account of Virginia Hill's appearance at the Kefauver hearings. Lacey learned the story from a veteran American newspaperman, Harold Conrad. Conrad got the story from the horse's mouth—one of Kefauver's top aides, who was in the hearing room at the time.

Virginia Hill Hauser (her married name) appeared before the Kefauver

Virginia Hill

Charles Tobey

Committee on March 15, 1951. Hill had been Bugsy Siegel's lover and collaborator until the gangster's murder in 1949. Before taking up with Siegel, she had been a top Mob courier, running money and messages between New York and Chicago. Kefauver hoped Hill would spill the secrets she had carried.

Hill was born in Lipscomb, Alabama, in 1916, where she grew up dirt poor, one of ten siblings. By 1933, when she was seventeen, she had become a stunning beauty. Wearing what she claimed was the first pair of shoes she ever owned, she left home for Chicago to work at the World's Fair. In Chicago she became—accounts differ—a waitress, a dancer, or a prostitute. Whichever trade she plied, Joe Epstein, then a senior and well-connected bookmaker, was one of her customers. Epstein took a shine to the beautiful teenager and took her under his wing. He set her up with an apartment, taught her social graces, and supported her. He also introduced her to the upper echelons of American mobsters: Joe Adonis, Frank Nitti, Charles Fischetti, Frank Costello—all were Hill's lovers. Epstein remained Hill's benefactor throughout. Some claim that, just before Bugsy Siegel's murder, Epstein put his protégée on a plane to Paris, thereby saving her life.

As with many Kefauver witnesses, Virginia Hill was summoned to appear before the Committee first in a closed morning session. The senators used these sessions to preview the testimony and thereby ascertain the best questions to ask once the TV cameras were on in the afternoons. They found Hill hostile and uncooperative. However, the Committee members

established that she had received substantial sums of money from men over the years, particularly from Epstein. Senator Charles Tobey demanded to know why.

Charles W. Tobey was the oldest member of the Kefauver Committee and its self-appointed Christian conscience. The senior Republican senator from New Hampshire was born in 1880 and raised a devout Baptist. His mother forbade card playing, theatregoing and the reading of Sunday papers. Tobey considered himself the better for it. He carried a Bible with him at all times, and frequently flavoured his comments with passages of scripture. He wore a translucent green eyeshade against the TV lights.

Tobey pressed Hill on which men gave her money and why. Hill was evasive. Tobey homed in on the support she received, year after year, from Joe Epstein. Why, when he was old enough to be her father, would Epstein do that? Tobey demanded. Hill smouldered. Tobey pressed on, his questioning ending with this exchange:

SENATOR TOBEY: But why would he give you all that money?

WITNESS: Senator, you don't want to know.

SENATOR TOBEY: Yes, I do. I want to know.

WITNESS: You really want to know?

SENATOR TOBEY: Yes.

WITNESS: Then I'll tell you why. Because I'm the best cock sucker in America.

SENATOR KEFAUVER: Order! I demand order!

That, I believe, in fact I am sure of it, is the story my father told that day in 1956, while I waited outside the locked door of his office with my tray of coffees from the Barclay Hotel kitchen. I have since found the incident reported in a half-dozen books and articles. However, when I filed a request to the Library of Congress for a transcript, I was told it was unavailable. The file of that particular session, they informed me, has disappeared.

IN THE END, the Kefauver Committee did nothing to impede organized crime. What Kefauver did do was ride from town to town like a latter-day Paul Revere, raising the alarm that the Mafia was coming—and bookmaking was paying its way. A Two Dollar Bet Means Murder! exclaimed the title of one popular anti-gambling tract. Suddenly wagering was no longer a petty sin conducted with a neighbourhood scofflaw; two-dollar bets now

lined the pockets of Frank Costello, the Prime Minister of the Underworld, who used the money to underwrite the rest of the Mafia's crimes. But—the argument continued hopefully—if gambling was the Mafia's cash cow, it was also its Achilles' heel: stop the bookmaking and organized crime would starve. It was a theory that had been circulating through law-enforcement circles for a decade, propagated tirelessly by Virgil T. Peterson and his network of crime commissions. Through the 1940s it gathered momentum until it became so ubiquitous that most law enforcers, above and below the 49th parallel, mistook it for true. In Ontario, Inspector Charlie Scott, Crown Attorney J. W. McFadden and their fellow lawmen already knew that instantaneous race information was crucial to the bookies. Now they realized that it was equally important to the Mafia. To prevent organized crime from gaining a foothold in the province, all they had to do was cut the race wire. They could keep the Mafia out of Ontario by putting Davy Bossin in jail.

• • • 13. The only game in town • • •

ON APRIL 14, 1942, George Drew, the leader of the Conservative Party of Ontario, rose from his bench in the Ontario Legislature. Waving a report by the Toronto Presbytery of the United Church of Canada, he rebuked Premier Mitch Hepburn for tolerating 'racketeering on a scale never before known in Canada, taking place right around us'. He was referring to the gambling clubs on the outskirts of Toronto. In particular, he pointed to Manny Feder's Combine Club, which he said should be 'dynamited and blown out of existence'. He called Feder 'the Overlord of the Underworld' and went on, 'I despise Manny Feder and all of his kind. I am a Canadian and I will not stop in my attempts to rid Canada of rats of this type.' According to the *Star*, the chamber broke into applause.

Drew did not mention Davy in his remarks that day and had probably never heard of him, but it was Drew's speech that began the chain of events that would finally force my father out of the race-wire business.

Manny Feder, Drew's 'Overlord of the Underworld' and his wife Frances were friends of my parents. I recall a photo of the four of them standing in front of the Feders' Tudor mansion at their farm in Temperance, Ontario, a few miles northwest of Toronto. For Manny, the *goldene medina* had certainly fulfilled its promise.

The Feders had come to Canada from Poland when Manny was a child, a few years after the Bossins. Like Davy, Manny became a newsboy, but unlike my father he stayed in school and graduated high school with honours. He might have continued on to university and a legitimate career, but his father died suddenly, and Manny and his brothers left school to work. They ran crap games and made book. With his quick mind, considerable charm, and a liberal use of bribery, Manny rose rapidly in the gambling business. For a time, it was rumoured that the police acted as Manny's strongmen, busting independent bookies who did not chip in their share of the monthly payoffs Manny arranged. Feder himself maintained an unblemished criminal record until 1936, when at age twenty-six he was accused of conspiring to fix a horse race. He was acquitted. By then the Feder brothers had built the Atlas Sporting Club on Lakeshore Boulevard

in Etobicoke, just west of the Toronto city limits. Popularly known as the Brown Derby, the club was the city's pre-eminent gambling joint. When the streetcar stopped near its entrance, the conductor would simply announce 'Brown Derby'. What Harry Ship famously boasted about his casino in Montreal—'Name me a prominent citizen who does *not* come here'—Manny could have said of the Brown Derby.

However, that era was drawing to a close. As in the United States, the rapprochement between Ontario's gamblers and the authorities eroded as the 1930s wound down. Heavily Protestant Ontario had always been home to a more robust anti-gambling movement than Catholic Quebec or the rough-and-tumble Western provinces. While some Ontario officials had been content to look the other way (with or without inducements), graft in Toronto was never as pronounced or systematic as it was in Halifax, Montreal or Vancouver. The Ontario leaders and authorities tended to share the anti-gambling ethic of the province's Protestant churchmen, or at least they pretended to. While it was widely believed that the gambling industry contributed heavily to the Liberals—Lionel 'Big Train' Conacher, the hockey and football star who became a Liberal Member of Provincial Parliament, was reputed to be the bagman—Premier Hepburn himself proudly announced, 'I have never been on a race track except when Their Majesties the King and the Queen were here, and I have never been in a gambling joint in my life.' Hepburn's Attorney General, Gordon Conant added, 'Personally or officially, I make no excuse for gambling in any form—nations that countenance it openly never rise to very great heights.' What Conant thought of Great Britain, where gambling was openly countenanced, is unrecorded.

The Chief Constable of Toronto, Dennis Draper, was another staunch foe of gaming. Draper was incorruptible, which even his detractors acknowledged. Though many condemned the longtime chief as a martinet, and a few criticized his obsession with Communists, unionists and Jews (whom he equated), no one ever doubted Draper's probity or, over-all, that of his force. So the captains of the gambling industry—Abe Orpen, Bill Beasley, Willie Morrissey, and Manny Feder—fled Toronto for its suburbs, where the local constabularies were small and the municipal politicians welcoming.

However, on June 15, 1938, without informing the Etobicoke Police Commission (and thereby risking a tip-off), a raiding party of provincial constables from Hamilton, Kitchener and Niagara Falls descended on the

Brown Derby. The hand-picked squad raided at supper time, when the club's more respectable (and prominent) customers were likely to be home having dinner with their families. Manny Feder, himself, was not at the club. He was arrested by Charlie Scott at his suite at the Royal York Hotel. As he was being hustled into the paddy wagon, Manny attempted to drop a key from his pocket down the sewer, but he missed the grate and Scott recovered the key. It opened a safety deposit box at the hotel, which contained $6,850 and several boxes of 'loaded' dice. Scott claimed the dice would not land on 7 or 11. Whether this was so, and whether such chicanery went on at the Brown Derby, was never resolved. Manny had a reputation for running an honest game. Who was to be believed, the boss gambler or the head of the anti-gambling squad? It came down to personal preference. The accusation did not diminish attendance at Feder's crap tables—recalling Canada Bill Jones' oft-quoted answer when he was warned that a game in which he was playing was rigged. 'I know,' the legendary nineteenth-century riverboat gambler replied, 'but it is the only game in town.'

Raids like the one on the Brown Derby had always occurred from time to time. Abe Orpen's National Sporting Club and Bill Beasley's casino had been similarly hit over the years. The proprietors were fined, and the clubs were back in business in short order. But Orpen and Beasley were not Jews. Feder was, and he was sentenced to four months in jail. In fact, the evidence against Manny was sketchy—everyone knew he ran the Brown Derby, but the proof offered in court was weak. Magistrate Hossack, who tried the case, was not, however, the same kind of stickler for evidence as Magistrate Forsythe, the presiding judge in the *Canadian Racing and Financial News* trial. Manny's lawyer, E.J. 'Eddy' Murphy launched an appeal, but it was suddenly dropped. Years later, Eva Feder, Manny's sister-in-law, told me that Manny withdrew the appeal in exchange for having all charges dropped against his brother, Phil. At the time Phil and Eva had young children; Manny and Frances were childless. (Manny had a reputation for that sort of generosity. After the Brown Derby raid, he collected the names of everyone in the Toronto police holding cells at the same time he was. When he paid his bail, he paid all of theirs as well.)

The Brown Derby never re-opened. Instead the Feders built the larger and more sumptuous Combine Club. That was the operation George Drew decried in 1942. When confronted by reporters with Drew's charges, Feder responded, 'I am trying to live down my past and forget it all. I invite

Colonel Drew to come out and see what I am doing these days. I have my farm here, 320 acres with over forty head of cattle. He can help me milk the cows.'

While Drew's attack failed to 'rid Canada of rats' of the Manny Feder 'type', it gave a sharp boost to Drew's own career, helping him to win the 1943 election. But once in power, Drew instigated no action against the Overlord of the Underworld. After 1943, Manny's name only made the papers when he hosted the county plowing matches, or when horses he bred were entered in major races. He died in 1947, following a stroke. He was just thirty-seven.

THOUGH GEORGE DREW'S 1942 crusade had little impact on the fortunes of the Feders, it would greatly influence the fortunes of the Bossins. Drew's charges, insubstantial as they were, made headlines and stung the Hepburn Liberals. Premier Hepburn was a hard-drinking womanizer who enjoyed the conviviality of the sporting crowd. But by 1942 rumours of his profligacy were catching up to him. In the face of Drew's attack, Hepburn and Attorney-General Gordon Conant became vigorous opponents of gambling. They hastily ordered the Ontario Provincial Police to organize a provincial anti-gambling squad, empowered to carry out raids regardless of the jurisdiction of local governments and police commissions. The squad, under the command of Inspector Edward T. Doyle, one of the top officers in the Ontario Provincial Police, hit the ground running. In the first month, the anti-gambling squad racked up 74 prosecutions, resulting in 59 convictions. They busted men playing dominoes and women gathered for a ladies' poker night. They impounded two slot machines found in the back of a convenience store. The machines were illegal under federal law but had been duly licensed by the township. The owner of the store was a member of the town council.

And so on. Inspector Doyle announced proudly that the squad's first raid, which closed down a gambling house in Fort Erie, marked the beginning of a new era in law enforcement. Indeed it did, but Doyle erred in saying the Fort Erie raid was the anti-gambling squad's first. In fact, their first raid was on 16 Royal York Rd., where my father sat at his switchboard, giving out the racing news.

• • • 14. Gentlemen's agreement • • •

The most notorious bookmaker in Toronto operated just beyond the city limits in an ordinary suburban house at 16 Royal York Road in Mimico. When the newly created provincial Anti-Gambling Squad raided this location in 1942, it discovered 56 telephone lines and a telegraph line going into the house. Attempts to have these lines removed were stymied, and when federal officials refused to take action, the provincial police finally got Bell Telephone to remove the lines. Homeowner, David Boskin then appealed to the Dominion Board of Transportation Commissioners. — Suzanne Morton, *At Odds: Gambling and Canadians 1919–1969*.

THOUGH PROFESSOR MORTON has mistaken my father's name and profession—he was never actually a bookie—she is right about the notoriety of the service he operated out of 16 Royal York Road. As soon as the Ontario Provincial Police (OPP) Anti-gambling Squad was formed in the spring of 1942, it was on Davy like a dog on a bone.

The first raid took place on May 6. Staff Inspector Edward Doyle submitted a detailed report:

... Knocking on the side entrance door I heard a man's voice exclaiming that there were two strange looking men at the door. The door was locked. It was opened by the man who made the remark, David Bossin.

The room contained three switchboards and a small turret board. In between the switchboards was a table that had telegraph equipment attached. Messrs Bossin and [blacked out] operated the switchboards and throughout the afternoon announced over the telephone the number of the first, second and third horse in each race, together with the peri mutual [sic] price paid at the track for the winning horse. Throughout the afternoon at intervals it was noted that calls were received by Bossin regarding the Provincial Police and Bossin would reply the police were keeping them company this afternoon.

Mr Bossin refused absolutely to answer any question.

The May 6 raid was followed by another the next day, and then by five more in early June, four over the summer, and a string of twelve raids in eleven days between September 29 and October 9. By this time Davy was threatening to sue not only the Ontario Provincial Police but Doyle himself.

Inspector Doyle took the evidence he had collected to Crown Attorney McFadden. But McFadden was still humbled by the failure of the *Canadian Racing and Financial News* case. He told Doyle, 'It might be better if this place could be put out of business in some other way than by means of pressing charges.' What way he had in mind was not indicated.

Though disappointed that the Crown was unwilling to prosecute, Doyle was undaunted, and he had a new idea. He approached the Wartime Prices and Trades Board, and suggested that they confiscate Davy's telephone equipment for war use. Again Doyle was disappointed. There was, the Board told him, no wartime shortage of phone equipment. Still, the Board expressed sympathy for the police effort, and promised to act on Doyle's request—as soon as he had obtained a conviction. Once again, the same obstruction blocked Doyle's path: it was frustratingly difficult to stop someone from doing something that had not been judged illegal.

So the nuisance raids on the *Weekly Sportsman* proved just that, a nuisance. They disrupted Davy's business but could not close it down. However, by the fall of 1942 Doyle had thought of a new angle.

I attended the office of Mr Rowe, the Toronto Manager of the Bell Telephone Company and there we discussed the question of the Royal York Road telephones....

Mr Rowe informed us that if the Honourable Attorney-General would order the service discontinued, action would be taken.

Doyle was excited. The phone company, it appeared, would cut off Davy's phone service if the Attorney General told it to—no conviction necessary. Doyle hurried back to report the news to the OPP commissioner, William Stringer. This might be, Doyle suggested, just what was needed to put Davy out of business 'some other way than by means of pressing charges.' They would, in effect, be deputizing the Bell Telephone Company—not exactly standard procedure, but a strategem that just might succeed where the police and the courts had failed.

Commissioner Stringer agreed. He wrote to Gordon Conant, Ontario's Attorney-General, urging him to issue an order that Bell Telephone could enact. The Attorney-General was intrigued. He invited the president of the Bell Telephone Company to meet with him.

The meeting took place in Toronto on October 1, 1942. Present were Attorney General Conant, his deputy C.L. Snyder, and the president of the Bell Telephone Company, C.F. Sise. They roughed out a gentlemen's agreement to discontinue the phone service to 16 Royal York Road. Conant left Snyder and the phone company president to work out the details. A week later, Snyder sent Sise what he considered to be the order the phone company needed. His letter concluded:

You are, therefore, advised that the telephone service you supply to No. 16 Royal York Road has the effect of permitting the occupants of these premises to contravene the provisions of the Criminal Code. In view of the fact that you are now given official notice of the use to which these telephones are put, your attention is also directed to the provisions of Section 69 of the Criminal Code.

This letter is sent to you in the belief that an organization as large and as important as the Bell Telephone Company of Canada will assist in the maintenance of law and order, the prevention of crime and the administration of justice.

Snyder's reference to Section 69 of the Criminal Code was a thinly veiled threat. Section 69 covered aiding and abetting a crime. The Deputy Attorney General of Ontario was warning the Bell Telephone Company that, if it allowed Davy to continue to use its telephone lines, the phone company itself could then be charged with aiding and abetting bookmaking.

President Sise was livid. He sent an immediate and sharp response to Conant:

... Mr Snyder's letter is not in any way in accordance with (our) understanding, namely that you were to request this Company to remove the telephone apparatus.... [Your letter] concludes that we are now given *official notice* of the use to which these telephones are put ... but there is no request from the Attorney-General for us to remove the apparatus, which is what we require before acting.

As stated plainly to Mr Snyder, this Company has not the right to pick and choose its customers. Under the law it must furnish service to any person applying for it. We wish to co-operate fully with law-enforcing authorities, but we cannot act without a specific request.

It took a week for the Ontario authorities to decide how to respond to Sise's rebuff. Attorney General Conant was a fastidious lawyer. He had not been present when Snyder and Sise agreed that the Attorney General would 'request' that Bell discontinue the phone service to 16 Royal York Road. Conant neither would, nor could, issue such a request. On what basis could the chief legal officer of the province demand cutting off the telephone service of someone who had not broken the law? Snyder had attempted to get around the problem by 'advising' Bell and 'giving notice', hoping the euphemisms would be understood as the required request. It had not worked because Bell Telephone was in the same boat as the Attorney General. It could not act against a customer on mere 'advice' even if it came from the Attorney General. It would only carry out an order, but no such order had been issued.

It was a conundrum. Snyder, however, had an idea for a way out: punt the responsibility back to the commissioner of the Ontario Provincial Police, who had proposed the approach to begin with. Snyder wrote to Commissioner Stringer. Stringer was happy to oblige, though he too felt constrained to word his letter to the telephone company delicately. On October 16, he wrote to Bell's Toronto office reporting that the OPP was 'satisfied' that the phones at 16 Royal York Road were being used for an illegal purpose. He requested that they be removed.

Though Stringer's letter was not everything Sise had hoped for—or agreed to—the president of Bell Telephone decided to interpret the police commissioner's request as the order from the Attorney General he needed. The phone company would go ahead and act on the basis of the

gentlemen's agreement. That evening at 8 p.m., Davy's phone lines went dead.

FOUR DAYS LATER, on October 22, the Board of Transport Commissioners of Canada—then the regulator of the telephone industry—received a notice from Thomas Agar, K.C., attorney for David Bossin. Agar demanded the Board order the phone company to reinstate Davy's telephone service. His application included this sentence:

Mr Bossin informs us that, to the best of his knowledge and belief, he is conducting his business on said premises in a lawful and legal manner, and he takes the position, and we also take it now on his behalf, that if he is not conducting his business in a lawful and legal manner but is, on the other hand, violating the provisions of the Criminal Code or of any other law in force in this country, he is subject to prosecution, and the proper course for the authorities to take is to commence such prosecution, but that if, on the other hand, he is, as he claims to be, conducting his business in a lawful and legal manner, it is contrary to the principles of British Justice for the Commissioner of Police of Ontario to adopt the novel procedure of requesting the Bell Telephone Company to remove from said premises the said telephones, and it is still more novel and unreasonable, on this basis, for the Bell Telephone Company to act upon such request.

After that 176-word sentence, Agar demanded an interim order restoring Davy's phone lines. The Board refused. It set the date for a hearing two weeks hence, on November 9, 1942.

THE BELL TELEPHONE COMPANY chose R.H. Greer, K.C., to argue its case before the Transportation Board. But Greer had a problem. Bell's position was that the request from Commissioner Stringer compelled it to act; the Company was in no position to second-guess the OPP and the Attorney General of Ontario, or to sift for itself the evidence of Davy's purported law-breaking. Bell was only following orders. When the province spoke, Bell Telephone had no choice but to do as it was told.

But therein was the rub: having taken the position that it was none of his business Greer could not turn around and defend his client by introducing evidence that Davy was aiding and abetting bookies. However, somebody had to—how else would the commissioners know what was really going on at 16 Royal York Road? Somehow, Greer had to get the

commissioners themselves to request the evidence that 'satisfied' the OPP that the phones needed to be removed. Or he had to get Davy on the witness stand, where he could be cross-examined on why he needed fifty-six telephone lines in the basement of a bungalow.

Greer wrote to Attorney General Conant, explaining his difficulty and requesting that the Attorney General's office compile the evidence against Davy, and be prepared to present it to the Transportation Board. He urged Conant to subpoena all Davy's records and publications. 'I have no doubt,' Greer wrote, 'that Bossin has not published a sheet of paper of any merit that the Board would pay any attention to.'

TWO DAYS LATER, on November 4, Davy received a subpoena demanding 'all books, papers, letters, publications, copies of letters and other writings and documents in your custody.'

The hearing was five days away.

• • • 15. *Omnia praesumuntur rite* • • •

THE BOARD OF TRANSPORT Commissioners met to hear the Bossin case on November 9, 1942, in an oak-panelled courtroom on the second floor of Toronto's City Hall, overlooking the former premises of Playfair Brown's horse room. It was a grey, cold day, threatening rain.

Thomas Agar's opening argument on behalf of my father was brief. He presented the contract for the telephone equipment at 16 Royal York Road. He noted that Davy had paid all his bills. He cited the statute that obliged Bell Telephone to provide phone service. Then he sat down.

R.H. Greer, for the Bell Telephone Company, rose and demanded more of Agar. The onus, he argued, should be on the plaintiff to explain why he needed fifty-six telephone lines. It should not be on the phone company for interrupting the service at the request of the Crown.

Then Greer pointed to a clause in the phone company's contract with Davy. It read, 'The undersigned applicant certifies that the service applied for is required for the purpose of carrying on a business as a publisher, which the applicant is lawfully entitled to do, and he undertakes that the service and facilities furnished by the Bell Telephone Company shall not be used for the transmission of messages conveying information relating to bookmaking, pool-selling, betting or wagering or intending to assist therein, or for any other unlawful purpose of whatever kind or nature.' This was a clause Bell routinely inserted into its service contracts where the equipment or set-up was suspicious. 'The Bell Telephone Company of Canada does not want to give service to bookmakers,' Greer told the Commissioners. 'The company is a law-abiding citizen of Canada. It cherishes its reputation.'

Greer then, gingerly, alluded to the evidence he could not introduce. 'We have not had the opportunity of hearing Mr Bossin explain why fifty-six wires should be used day to day, from the basement of a bungalow out in the country. We have not seen his newspaper, which he alleges he uses for the purpose of disseminating whatever he disseminates over all these wires. Issues of the *Weekly Sportsman* are not before you to see whether, in your opinion, they would justify the use of fifty-six wires. I suggest to you

that Mr Bossin might take away a lot of the darkness surrounding this case by coming forward and showing that he is not operating a bookmaking business. I believe the onus is on Mr Bossin to come here and produce his papers and establish his need for the fifty-six phone lines. The onus should not be on the Bell Telephone Company to show the negative.'

In fact, Greer told the Commission, Bell Telephone had been threatened with prosecution by the Attorney General of Ontario, and the president of the company had travelled from Montreal to Toronto to meet with him. At that meeting, Greer explained, they 'came to a gentlemen's agreement to carry out the Attorney General's request. In view of the sanctity of the office of the Attorney General, we feel it is our duty, if requested to do certain things, to do it.

'So we proceeded at the written request of the Attorney General and the Commissioner of Police. Rightly or wrongly, it is entirely on the strength of these two letters that the telephone company acted in disconnecting Mr Bossin's service. We have no knowledge ourselves that Mr Bossin has used our service or facilities unlawfully or that he intends to use them unlawfully in the future. The Bell Telephone Company has no police or judicial power, and it would not be in the public interest that we should.'

But, he suggested, pointedly, 'If the Board has questions with regard to Mr Bossin's activities or with regard to the reason the Attorney General sought the assistance of the telephone company, my friend, Mr Common, is here to answer them.'

W.B. Common, K.C., represented the Attorney General of Ontario at the hearing. He rose to address the Board. Thomas Agar, Davy's lawyer, objected. The issue before the Board, Agar argued, was between the Bell Telephone Company and his client. Bell Telephone was not accusing Davy of law-breaking. The Attorney General's opinions, whatever they were, were irrelevant.

'I think,' the Chief Commissioner ruled, 'if for no other or stronger reason, we would always hear the Attorney General upon his request.' W.B. Common then addressed the Board. 'Let me assure my friend,' he began, 'that I am not here to ask the Board to try the guilt or innocence of Mr Bossin. That is a matter for another tribunal. However, I respectfully submit that the Board should be seized of the evidence which is in the possession of the Crown authorities. It was on the request of the Crown authorities that the service to this residence was discontinued. So it

occurred to me, the Board might be interested in knowing the facts and circumstances which inspired the request.'

The Chief Commissioner replied to Common that, indeed, the Commission was interested about one point in particular. 'I think,' he said, 'we might be interested to know upon what authority, if any there was, the Commissioner of Provincial Police instructed the Bell Telephone Company to discontinue the service.'

Common answered that 'such a request by the Crown authorities, either the Attorney General for this Province or the Commissioner of Police, requires no statutory authority or other executive authority.' He continued, 'Commissioner Stringer merely made a request, as an officer charged with the enforcement of the law and the suppression and prevention of crime. It was his opinion that the Criminal Code was being violated and, as a means of preventing a further breach, he made a request to the Bell Telephone Company to discontinue the telephone service. The Bell Telephone Company acceded to that request. It did not have to, but for reasons it thought best, it did.'

'That is to say,' the Chief Commissioner replied, clarifying the point, 'the request of the Commissioner of Police was not supported by any statutory authority or order-in-council, or anything of that nature.'

'None at all,' Common conceded, 'other than the Commissioner's own appointment to that position.'

The exchange continued:

CHIEF COMMISSIONER: And to this time, no information has been laid against Mr Bossin.

MR COMMON: In all frankness before the Board, there is not sufficient evidence available to justify an information being laid at this stage. An information might be laid in the future.

CHIEF COMMISSIONER: In view of that, you would not want us to go into a sort of review of that matter now.

MR COMMON: I am not suggesting this tribunal should proceed on the merits as between the Crown and Bossin. That is not, of course, your jurisdiction, but I did feel that I should have available to the Board the evidence which, as I say, inspired our request to the Bell Telephone Company. So far, there is nothing before the Board as to the nature of the business which was conducted by Mr Bossin. For instance, I have a copy of the newspaper. My friend alleges in his application that his client is a publisher. I have a copy of the so-called publication, and I am

prepared to attack the *bona fides* of my friend's client's business, if the Board is interested. Of course that is up to the Board. I have the evidence and the witnesses here. The furthest I could ask the Board to go would be to hear the evidence, and to determine on it, not as to the guilt or innocence of Mr Bossin, but whether or not the Bell Telephone Company was justified, and still is justified, in discontinuing the service.

CHIEF COMMISSIONER: That is our difficulty. Sometimes one gets into embarrassing positions by trying to be helpful.

MR COMMON: Trying to carry out a gentlemen's agreement is sometimes very embarrassing.

CHIEF COMMISSIONER: However, we do not have to decide that.

He then turned to Davy's lawyer, Thomas Agar.

THOMAS AGAR, K.C. was one of Ontario's preeminent barristers. He had been called to the bar in 1905, the year my father was born. When he took Davy's case, he had been practising law for thirty-seven years.

I met Agar once, when I was very young, five or six years old. He was portly and bald with a neatly trimmed and waxed moustache. Why I have remembered that over the years, I don't know. Perhaps there was some gravity in the man, or some deference towards him by my father, who, otherwise, never deferred to anyone. Agar's den, where I was left to colour while he and Davy talked, was filled with trophies, ribbons, paintings and framed photographs of racehorses.

This is what he said to the Transportation Board: 'Gentlemen, I must say again what I said at the beginning of this hearing: all there is before you is a contract and an application to have the service promised in the contract resumed. That is all. There has been some suspicion creeping into the record that my client is using the telephone for an illegal purpose. My answer to my friend is to say, "If the Attorney General suspects a criminal offence, let him go downstairs in this building and lay a charge before a magistrate in Criminal Court." In the meantime Mr Bossin is a citizen of this country who is entitled to telephone service. We are here today, the same as any merchant on Yonge Street, asking to have our telephone service restored, and we are entitled to expect the same treatment as any reputable, well-known merchant on Yonge Street would be expected to receive, when he shows that his telephone service has been discontinued on the request of a Crown officer, who says that he suspects that we are

committing an offence. I need not remind you that we are innocent until proved to be guilty in a proper court of competent jurisdiction and that no judgment in any case should rest on suspicion.

'I am sure that the members of this Board recall the words of Mr Justice Riddel when he said, "We sit not to declare the law as we think it should be, but as it has been laid down. We are not a court of morals, but a court of law." And it has been a principle of law for hundreds of years that all things are presumed to have been done rightly, and duly performed, until it is proved to the contrary. *Omnia praesumuntur rite et solemniter esse acta doneo probetur in contrarium.* However, my friends, who are here representing the Bell Telephone Company of Canada and the Attorney General of Ontario, would have you change the law, so that things are now presumed to be done wrongly, and only when a citizen can prove that they are not, does he gain the right to have a telephone.

'Are we to adopt this new principle that you are guilty until you prove yourself to be innocent? That is what my friend suggests. He says, "Come along now, Mr Bossin, and tell us the nature and extent of your business and show us that you are not guilty of an offence."

'However, if my friend were to have his way, think of the ramifications. I have before me the Annual Report of the Chief Constable of the City of Toronto for the year 1941. I find in it, for example, there were 136 prosecutions for keeping a common bawdy house, in respect of which 28, or 20 percent, were found not guilty. I find in 1941 there were 31 prosecutions for running a betting shop and that about 30 percent were found not guilty. I find there were 12 charges of keeping a common gaming house and, of those, 25 percent were found not guilty.

'Let us assume for the moment that this Board says, "We are not going to order Mr Bossin's telephone service to be resumed." My friend will go back with great pride and pleasure to the Attorney General and say, "Well, we have now a way to deal with these people who are charged with committing criminal offences for which they may use their telephones. If we cannot prove it, we will just serve a notice on the Bell Telephone Company, as per the Bossin case, and the Bell Telephone Company will take away their phones". And what is the result? The result is that, according to the 1941 figures, telephones will be taken out of the approximately 25 percent of premises where the occupants were found not guilty.

'Just think of the intolerable situation in which the Ontario public is going to be, if I do not succeed in my application. Every merchant, every

department store, every citizen is going to be at the mercy of a Crown officer who has tried to get evidence for a conviction, and has failed to do so.

'My client uses fifty-six telephones for the purpose of giving information to members of the public who want it and I say, as a lawyer of thirty-seven years' experience, in so doing he is not violating any law, criminal or otherwise. If you walk out of this courtroom now and go across the street to Eaton's department store, or if you telephone some of the most outstanding merchants in this city and say, "Hello Mr So-and-so, do you sell any roulette tables?" you will get the reply, "Yes. We have a good one in our window. Would you like to come over and see it?" And if you do, is the vendor going to be obliged to find out from you why you are buying it? The law is that he can sell it, and if the purchaser uses it for an unlawful or criminal purpose, then the Crown has its deputies to go after him.

'David Bossin is within the law in doing what he is doing. Yet he has been under a state of persecution for months, with search warrants, with officers out there in his premises yet, and there has been no evidence collected to justify a charge. Mr Commissioners, there is not one scratch of a pen to indicate that my client is guilty of anything.

'Are you going to allow this Board to be the medium through which the Attorney General can act on mere suspicion? Are we going to allow the Attorney General to be judge, jury and everything else? That cannot be the law. I believe nothing more needs to be said.'

The hearing concluded without Davy saying a word.

ON DECEMBER 7, 1942, a month after Davy's application, the Board of Transport Commissioners delivered its verdict.

The Chief Commissioner, Colonel J.A. Cross, wrote:

The discontinuance of the applicant's telephone service by the Bell Telephone Company was solely in consequence of certain letters received by it from the Deputy Attorney General and the Commissioner of Police of Ontario. Mr Common, representing the Attorney General, stated that, at the time of the hearing, there was not sufficient information available to justify an information being laid against Bossin in another Court. Mr Common also admitted that the letters referred to had only the effect of a request to the Company to discontinue the service, and that they were not supported by any statutory authority, Order-in-Council or

anything of that nature whereby the Company could be compelled to act upon the request.

In my opinion, the discontinuance of the service of the applicant constituted a breach by the Company of the contract for the furnishing of telephones and service. The Board directs the Company to restore to the applicant forthwith the telephone service which he received immediately prior to its discontinuance on the sixteenth day of October, 1942.

The twin principles that *omnia praesumuntur rite esse acta*, that all things are presumed to have been done rightly and that we are innocent until proven guilty, stood. The Transportation Board's ruling was a significant one, setting a precedent that has restricted both public officials and private companies when, in their zeal, they consider abrogating the rights of citizens. Because of the Bossin case, the authorities cannot, to this day, take away someone's telephone (or internet service) because they do not like what he is doing with it.

In later years, my father hated the telemarketers who always seemed to call at suppertime. He even phoned Bell Telephone to complain. He was told that the company could do nothing because of a ruling years before by the Board of Transport Commissioners.

WITH HIS TELEPHONE service restored, Davy went back to work, and the police went back to hounding him. And so it went for two more years, but then the Crown finally caught a break. Belatedly, a junior officer, onto whose desk the Bossin file had fallen, thought to check the zoning for the bungalow at 16 Royal York Road. The street, it turned out, was zoned residential. The *Weekly Sportsman*, whatever else it was or was not, was certainly a business, so its operation contravened the bylaw. Davy was charged, found guilty and fined $10. On the surface of it, it was an insect bite, but for Davy it was the last straw. There would be, he knew, more summonses, more convictions and more harassment. If he tried to set up elsewhere, he was unlikely to be given the telephone lines he needed, since wartime restrictions were still in place. In early 1945, Davy simply walked away from the racing information business.

It was, as it turned out, a prescient decision. The race wire's day was nearly done. In the end it was not thwarted by the authorities, whose might would continue to be overmatched by the public's desire for the information the race wire provided, and by the wiliness of the bookies in

providing it. What undid the wire was simply time and technology, as the telegraph gave way to the telephone, the walkie-talkie, the ubiquity of radio—some stations specialized in broadcasting immediate race results—and the advent of television. By the time the race wire was finally outlawed in the United States (by Robert Kennedy's 1961 *Interstate Wire Act*), no one had used it for years. Kennedy's law would rest on the books, derelict and unapplied, for the next forty years. Then in the new century it suddenly sprang up again, as a weapon against on-line gambling. Whether a law meant to outlaw one thing can be used to outlaw something else that was unforeseen when the law was drafted remains to be seen. The first Wire-Act convictions are still winding their way through the uncertain channels of judicial appeal.

WHEN HE ABANDONED his switchboard in 1945, Davy returned to laying off bets, if indeed he had ever fully stopped. Once again he walked from phone booth to phone booth, carrying on his business over the five miles from our house to the Royal York Hotel. A few more years and he would be out of the gambling business altogether.

THE MOST OUTRAGEOUS story I ever heard Davy tell was the one about how Irving 'Big Gangy' Cohen quit the underworld. Davy's stories frequently seemed too good to be true, and I have no doubt he shined them up some, as all story-tellers do. But about this one in particular, I always had my doubts. However, thanks to the internet, the doubts have been put to rest; this really happened.

In the early 1930s, Irving Cohen was a member of the Brownsville Gang, a tough bunch of young Jewish hoodlums from the Brownsville neighbourhood of Brooklyn. The gang had a hand in every type of crime practised in the Dirty Thirties, including gambling, loan-sharking, extortion and murder. Eventually, they formed the nucleus of Murder, Incorporated, as the press called Albert Anastasia's company of hit men.

Gangy Cohen and his friend Walter Sage joined the Brownsville boys in the late 1920s. The gang was happy to induct Cohen, who stood a head taller than his comrades and used his size and reach like a heavyweight fighter. Walter Sage's skills ran more to the actuarial, and he eventually ran the gang's slot machine business on Long Island. Sage's position made it easy for him to skim money from his less sophisticated comrades. Eventually, however, the gang realized what he was up to. In the harsh world of Brownsville, stealing from the gang was a capital offence. Sage's execution was ordered. To allay Walter's suspicions, Gangy Cohen was assigned to lure his friend out of town by inviting him to a party in the Catskills. At the appointed time, Cohen and two other gang members drove to Sage's house and picked him up. Walter got into the passenger seat with Gangy behind him in the back.

After they left the city, they drove down a wooded country road. Accounts differ as to what happened next, but it went something like this: on a signal from his seat mate, Cohen reached forward and pinned Walter Sage to the front seat. Sage was stabbed repeatedly with an ice pick. He did not die quickly and, flailing, kicked the steering wheel, sending the car swerving off the road. When it came to a stop, Sage was dead, slumped against the dashboard. Gangy Cohen threw open the back door and ran

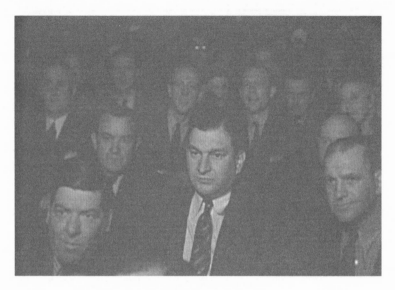

Big Gangy Cohen in *Golden Boy*

into the woods. The others assumed the grisly killing had loosened Cohen's bowels. They threw Sage's body into the trunk, and called to Gangy to hurry. There was no reply, and Cohen did not return. When repeated calls failed to bring him back, they left without him and drove to a nearby lake, where a rowboat had been stashed. Sage's body was hauled into the boat, and a slot machine lashed to it. They then dropped Walter Sage into the lake.

Gangy Cohen was not seen again by any of the Brownsville gang for two years. Then, in 1939, Abe 'Pretty' Levine went to the local Loews Theatre to see *Golden Boy*, the boxing movie with William Holden and Barbara Stanwyck. In one scene the camera lingered on the intent faces of the gamblers at ringside, and there on the screen was Big Gangy Cohen. Levine rushed back to his friends to tell them what he had seen. Bets were placed, and the gang headed back to the theatre. Sure enough, it was Big Gangy Cohen.

Not long after that, Pretty Levine was arrested. By then, Pretty had a young wife and a sixteen-month-old daughter, and he wanted out of the gangster life. The Brooklyn District Attorney, Burton Turkus, sensed the weakness in his prisoner. He had Mrs Levine arrested and put in the Women's House of Detention, and sent the child to an orphanage. Turkus told Pretty he would personally make sure they stayed there, if Levine

didn't talk. He did. Among his revelations, he told the story of Sage's murder, putting the ice pick in Cohen's hand. He then told Turkus about seeing Gangy in *Golden Boy*. (In another version of the story, it was a New York policeman who went to the movies and saw Cohen playing a cop. He recognized him from his photograph on the station's wanted posters.) Cohen was arrested in California and extradited to New York for trial.

In Cohen's version of the murder, he had not wielded the ice pick, in fact, he had himself been stabbed in the arm in the melee, whereupon he wondered if he too had been set up. At that moment, he had a revelation: even if he was not targeted this time, his turn would come eventually. So he ran for it, and kept running. At dawn, he made his way to a town where he caught a bus, the first leg of a journey taking him as far away from Brownsville as he could get. That turned out to be Los Angeles. There, another émigré from the old neighbourhood, Slapsie Maxie Rosenbloom, got him a job as a bit player in gangster movies.

Cohen's trial for the murder of Walter Sage was a shambles. The accounts of what went on were so discrepant and the witnesses so unreliable that the jury threw up its hands and acquitted Gangy Cohen. He returned to Hollywood, where he again played minor movie roles. After the gangster genre went out of fashion, Gordon's size continued to guarantee him work as a bad guy or a cop. In 1959 he found a steady job as the double for Hoss Cartwright on the TV series *Bonanza*. Cohen died peacefully in the mid-1970s. His grandchildren remember him fondly, and have contributed their own recollections to the internet discussion of his life.

My father enjoyed the tale of Big Gangy Cohen's epiphany as much as his listeners—Davy was a great one for laughing at his own stories—but I never knew him to tell a story for that reason alone. There was always a moral. In this case it was that the underworld is easy to enter but hard to escape. Gangy Cohen realized it, and made a break for it. Davy did too.

'YOUR FATHER was the smartest man I ever met', one of Davy's friends told me. That his criminal record consisted of one ten-dollar zoning violation in a quarter century of law-breaking seems pretty smart to me. And so was his decision to get out when he did.

By 1950, not only was the race wire going the way of the horse-and-carriage, but the temper of the times had changed. Whipped up by the Kefauver Committee's televised accusations, hysteria about the boss gamblers was rampant. Crackdowns were everywhere. Frank Erickson, my

father's top layoff connection, was finally convicted of bookmaking. Erickson had been busted dozens of times over the years, but none of the charges ever stuck. However, in 1950, he testified candidly at the hearings of a U.S. Senate Committee investigating the race wire. He was granted immunity from federal prosecution, but New York State was not bound by the deal, and it took the opportunity to finally put Erickson in jail, based on his 'confession'. He served ten months.

Frank Costello would soon follow him to prison, for contempt of Congress. After days of interrogation by the Kefauver Committee, Costello asked for a postponement due to ill health. He provided a doctor's letter stating that his throat was badly inflamed.[1] Kefauver refused to delay the proceedings. Incensed, Costello walked out. For that, he was sentenced to eighteen months in prison. While he served the sentence, he was prosecuted for tax evasion. Though the auditors only came up with $51,000 in untaxed income spread over four years, Costello was convicted and the judge gave him the maximum sentence, five years in jail. He was sixty-three.

In March 1957, after serving a year, Costello was released on bail while his case was appealed. Two months later, as he walked into his apartment building, a man came up behind him and said, 'Frank, this is for you.' Costello whirled around as the man shot him at point-blank range. Miraculously, the bullet only grazed his scalp. Seeing the blood spurting from Costello's head, the shooter fled. The would-be assassin was Vincent 'the Chin' Gigante, an enforcer for the ambitious Mafia chieftain Vito Genovese. Gigante was tried, but he was acquitted when Costello refused to identify him.

Genovese's gunman missed, but like Gangy Cohen, Costello could see which way the wind was blowing. The Prime Minister of the Underworld resigned, clearing the path for Genovese to become the undisputed boss of the New York Mob. Where Costello had been a diplomat and a fixer, Genovese was a thug. Such civility as there had been in the underworld rapidly deteriorated.

This was true in Toronto as well. Through the years Davy was in

1 Costello's characteristic hoarse whisper was the result of a botched throat operation. Marlon Brando imitated Costello's voice for his portrayal of Don Corleone in *The Godfather*.

the gambling business, Toronto had been, essentially, free of the Mafia. Montreal was a Mafia town, Hamilton was, and Buffalo was, but Toronto was not. The mobsters had been kept at bay by Chief Draper's hard-nosed and relatively honest police force, and by a local gambler, loan shark and *gonif*, Max Bluestein. Bluestein had such a reputation for violence that the out-of-towners gave him, and Toronto, a wide berth. But in March 1961, Johnny 'Pops' Papalia, the Hamilton mafioso, called Bluestein to a meeting at the Town Tavern, a popular downtown Toronto jazz club. There he made Bluestein an offer he couldn't refuse. Bluestein, however, did refuse. Confident that the Hamilton don would not risk a move in front of so many witnesses, Bluestein dismissed his entourage. As he got up to leave, Papalia and his men jumped him, beating him severely with brass knuckles, an iron bar and a broken bottle. They left him for dead. Over 100 witnesses claimed to have seen nothing. However, after a young, crusading *Star* columnist named Pierre Berton refused to let the story die, the Toronto police assigned a hand-picked team of the city's best detectives to the investigation. Papalia and his henchmen went to jail, but neither Bluestein nor Toronto was the same again.[2]

IN 1951, a dozen years before that night at the Town Tavern, Davy had quit the gambling business. He took the train to New York and went to see Frank Costello, to tell him he wanted out. My father taught me to always go to the top, and that is what he did. Davy was nervous about the trip (his brother reported this to me). Though he didn't need Costello's permission—my father was not 'connected'—he knew that going straight was a

2 Herb Thurston led the special team and told me how he cracked the case: he picked up a local hoodlum who had been at the Town Tavern that night. The man had himself been attacked by the Hamilton mobsters a year before. They had broken both his legs with a baseball bat. Thurston left his guest to sit alone in an interrogation room for several hours. Then he returned and explained that he was now going to drive him back to Spadina Avenue in a cruiser with the lights flashing. He would let him go with a great public display of thanks. 'But everyone will think I peached. Do you know what they'll do to me?' the shocked man exclaimed. 'You bet I do,' Thurston told him. 'If I were you, I'd start talking, starting with the names of everyone you saw at the Town Tavern that night.' Thurston thus developed a list of witnesses with whom he was equally persuasive.

tricky proposition, unbalancing the reciprocity that keeps law-breakers' secrets safe. Having the word out that Frank Costello had given his blessing was the best insurance there was.

Davy met Costello in the barbershop of the Waldorf Astoria, where 'Uncle Frank' held court. He told Costello his intention. 'It's not the same business anymore,' he said. Costello agreed and told Davy that, if he could, he would get out himself. He asked Davy what he was going to do. Davy told him he was starting a booking agency in Toronto. Costello wished him well, and said, if there was ever anything he could do, let him know. Then he added, 'But stay out of the United States.' To the best of my knowledge, my father never went there again. I know we never went to Disneyland, despite my best efforts to convince him to take me.

I ONCE ASKED my father why he quit when he did. He told me the business had gotten mean. Forty years later a friend of his told me that, around that time, a couple of hoods from the Maggadino crime family in Buffalo visited Davy at the Royal York. They told him their boss had decided to become Davy's partner. My father looked at his visitors and said nothing, in the same way he had with so many people for so many years. Then he picked up the phone and called the police. As the Maggadino emissaries listened, he asked for the morality squad. 'There are a couple of hoods sitting here,' he said into the phone, 'telling me Maggadino sent them to put the muscle on me.' Then Davy handed them the phone. The sergeant told them to be on the next train back to Buffalo; otherwise, they should plan on staying in Canada for the next ten years. They caught the train.

Another of Davy's friends offered his own explanation for Davy's decision to get out. He told me Davy quit because he was bored. 'Davy had a mind like a steel trap,' he said. 'That's why he loved the wire service. It fascinated him. It was cutting-edge technology, like computers are today. And he was working with a lot of very smart guys. Don't ever think the gambling business was run by a bunch of dummies, just because they didn't talk like college graduates. They created a hell of an industry—big, big money. How do you move all that money around? Think about it.

'When you are in business, any business, you have all sorts of problems to solve, something new, every day. It's exciting. For Davy, the race wire was like that. And he was fighting the most powerful people in the province, and beating them too. After that, how much fun could it be spending your days taking bets over the telephone?'

My mother had a different explanation for why Davy went straight, one, oddly enough, I had never thought of. She said, 'Honey, you were getting older and he didn't want you to grow up in that world. It wasn't about him. It was about you.'

———

From the diary of Prime Minister Mackenzie King, March 29, 1938:

'A very difficult question has presented itself in Roosevelt's appeal to [admit] refugees from Austria, Germany, etc. That means, in a word, admitting numbers of Jews. My own feeling is that nothing is to be gained by creating an internal problem in an effort to meet an international one. We must ... seek to keep this part of the Continent free from unrest and from too great an intermixture of foreign strains of blood.... One has to look at realities and meet these situations in the light of conditions, not theories.'

Davy's years in the gambling business coincided with the Great Depression, the Second World War and the Holocaust. That these three great twentieth-century upheavals are largely absent from this account reflects Davy's luck and disposition. He managed to escape all three.

Davy thrived through the Depression. The hard times of the 1930s meant good times for the gambling business. A quarter wagered on a horse was as cheap as entertainment got, and even with the odds against you, a bet held out more hope than the unemployment office. So the bookies prospered, and my father prospered with them.

He shared his wealth. Davy took to carrying a large roll of bills in his pocket, as Arnold Rothstein had, but unlike Rothstein who loaned out the money at usurious interest, Davy spread his good fortune among family, friends, and acquaintances down on their luck. He developed a reputation as a soft touch, which he countered with gruffness. Later, he would warn me never to loan anyone money, but then he would add, 'Any loan is a gift. If you get the money back, that's another gift. Any other way you look at it will drive you nuts.'

The Depression ended with the war. By the time Canada instituted conscription, Davy was nearly forty, well beyond draft age, and there was no way he was going to volunteer. His brothers did. My uncle Hye was turned down by the Canadian army because he only had nine toes. One had

been crushed by a cart and amputated when he was a child. My uncle Art, who was by then a screenwriter in Hollywood, joined the U.S. Third Infantry. He was one of the soldiers who overran Hitler's retreat at Berchtesgaden. There, amid the general looting, he 'liberated' a stack of the Führer's notepaper. For years, he used it as his personal stationery, augmenting the eagle-and-swastika emblem of the Third Reich with the words, 'Under new management.'

Hye and Art had been eager to join up; Davy would have none of it. He was not a man to take orders, and he was too cynical to trust the statesmen and the generals to make decisions in anyone's interest but their own. He was not disloyal; in his own way, he was grateful to Canada. Like all Canadian Jews of his generation, Davy was relieved, as he told me, 'to live in a country where you don't have to run for the border if the wrong guy gets in.' But that was no reason to kill or be killed on Mackenzie King's say-so. Before he would go to war, he said, he would head to the backwoods of Quebec with an axe. Coming from a man who could scarcely change a light bulb, it was a comical picture, but the sentiment was clear. I remember asking him why he did not want to be a soldier (I must have been very young), and he told me what his father told him: 'Why should a Jew fight for the Czar?' It was as close as he ever got to talking to me about the anti-Semitism that had dogged him all his life.

From the vantage point of the twenty-first century, it is hard to imagine the extent of anti-Semitism in Canada in the first half of the twentieth century. From 1920 on, Jews were effectively barred from immigrating. Those who had come earlier and established themselves, like the Bossins, found that apartment buildings would not rent to them. Banks, insurance companies, and other major employers would not hire them. My uncle Hye was turned down for a newspaper job because, they told him, they already had a Jewish reporter. Jews could attend university (though the University of Toronto Medical School kept racial quotas into the 1960s). However, when they graduated, Jewish doctors could not find internships. Schools would not hire Jewish teachers. Davy took up the gambling business because it was one of the few white-collar jobs open to him.

But for all that, Jewish families, including mine, took comfort in the relative civility of Canadian prejudice. To those who had only recently escaped the pogroms and persecutions of Europe, Canada in the 1920s was, all in all, a safe haven. But in the 1930s as Hitler ascended in Germany, anti-Jewish sentiment in Canada hardened. The Nazis' success emboldened

Canadian anti-Semites and, as they became more vocal, Mackenzie King's government, many of whom held their own antipathy to Jews, followed suit.[3] The worse things got for European Jews, the more firmly Canada locked and bolted its doors against them. Thousands of Jews, desperate to flee Nazi persecution, were turned away, even while their Canadian kin begged to sponsor them. Most did not survive. To the day he died, Davy never voted Liberal. I suspect this was the reason.

Over the years, Canada's complicity in the Holocaust has been swept under the rug, but it was well understood by Canadian Jews at the time.[4] Jewish organizations and individuals, including some of my relatives (though not so far as I know my father) campaigned desperately to soften Canada's position, but nothing they did (or could have done) had any effect. As Irving Abella and Harold Troper write in their exhaustive and disturbing study, *None Is Too Many: Canada and the Jews of Europe, 1933–1948*, 'The major and unavoidable flaw in the Canadian Jews' campaign was their assumption that a civilized world would not permit exactly what, in the end, it did permit.'

I grew up knowing none of this. Davy and Marci never said anything. I cannot recall when or how I eventually found out about the Holocaust. But once I did, I asked my parents if we had lost any relatives. They said no; everybody had left the Old Country years before. I believed that.

My parents' reticence is understandable. The massacre of six million Jews (and several million Roma, gays, leftists and others) was simply too painful, and too shameful, to talk about to a child. I remember noticing that

3 Frederick Blair, the head of King's Immigration Branch, compared the Jews' efforts to escape Europe to 'what I have seen on a farm at hog feeding time when they are all trying to get their feet in the trough.' This was Canada's top immigration policy-maker. When asked how many Jewish refugees Canada should accept, another Canadian official answered candidly and memorably, 'None is too many.'

4 I have not chosen the word 'complicity' lightly. Of all the western nations, Canada took in the fewest Jewish refugees of any country capable of providing sanctuary: a scant five thousand between 1933 and 1939 and only eight thousand more after the war. Worse, the King government urged other countries to adopt the same stance. Even when, in 1938 and 1939, Hitler offered to release any Jews other nations would accept, the offer was ignored, leaving the Nazis to devise their own 'final solution'.

the mother of one of my friends had a number tattooed on her arm. I asked why and got a cursory reply. Normally that would have set off a volley of questions; I was an inveterate *noodnik*, as my father would say, a pesterer. But that time I knew somehow to let the subject go, and I did. Most of the Jewish kids I knew grew up with the same kind of silence.

It was only when writing this book that I began to wonder if the Bossins had really come through the Holocaust as unscathed as I had always thought. So I called my cousin Benny who, you may recall, honeymooned at Yankee Stadium in 1947, courtesy of Davy and Frank Costello. Benny was born in Toronto in 1926, making him just old enough to have his own memories of the Nazi era. I asked him if, indeed, no Bossins had perished in Europe.

'Of course they did,' he said. 'Not our first cousins. They had all emigrated around the same time as Zussman, when Canada let Jews in. But there were others, sure. After the war, your Uncle Lou went back to see what he could find, but they were all gone, all dead.'

Benny recalled the fruitless attempts to move the Canadian government. From time to time as he did, he repeated like a refrain, 'But what could you do? You couldn't do anything.'

As our conversation neared its end, I remarked how much had changed in just a generation or two. Back then, I said, the anti-Semites ran the country; now they were reduced to a few fringe groups of neo-Nazis and Holocaust deniers. Just a half-century later, I said, we have the United Nations Declaration of Human Rights, the Charter of Rights and Freedoms, laws against hate crimes, human rights commissions.

Benny was silent a moment. I think he was deciding whether or not to reply. 'Bobby, I'll tell you something,' he said finally. 'If they had a chance, they'd stand you and me up against the wall and shoot us. They would do it in a minute. That fire never stops smouldering. It could break out again in an instant, and that's what would happen. We have to live with that. There's no such thing as Gentiles loving Jews. They never have and they never will.'

Twenty years younger, born after the events that had seared themselves into my cousin's memory, I groped for a reply. But I could think of none.

• • • 17. Sh-Boom • • •

RUBEN RIVAS ONCE TOLD ME, 'If Davy Bossin said, "You don't work,"
you didn't work.' Ruben was a young Latin bandleader my father discov-
ered a few years after he started his booking agency. He managed Ruben's
career from 1955 until his death in 1963. When Davy died, Ruben was dev-
astated. 'I loved him more than my own father,' he told me, which I took
with a grain of salt. Of course, teenage sons tend to be hard on their
fathers. As a kid, you see them as bigger than they are, then as smaller.
When you grow up, hopefully it evens out. It seemed to me that Ruben,
nursed by Davy through his apprenticeship in show business, was still at
the first stage. So when he said things like 'If Davy Bossin said, "You don't
work," you didn't work,' I thought, yeah-yeah, sure.

Davy had been offered his talent agency, Theatrical Attractions, as
payment for a gambling debt. Wanting out of the gambling business, he
accepted. He had always loved musicals, vaudeville and nightclubs, and he
took readily to his new line of work. Theatrical Attractions did well. Davy
booked Ella Fitzgerald, Sammy Davis Jr., Xavier Cugat. But the Ruben
Rivas Orchestra was the only act Davy managed. Being a manager is differ-
ent from being an agent. An agent books performances; a manager does
everything else. Before Ruben, Davy had managed one other act. Briefly.
That had ended badly.

RUBEN RIVAS had come to Toronto from Mexico in 1950 to study engi-
neering. He was seventeen. He supported himself by singing 'Cucurrucucu
Paloma', 'Malagueña Salerosa' and other Latin standards, accompanying
himself on flamenco guitar. Latin music was popular then—I remember, a
few years later, learning to cha-cha-cha—but the gigs were few in
Toronto, which was just emerging from the indigo of its blue laws. One
hungry, penniless lunchtime, Ruben walked into Basil's, the Yonge Street
restaurant and nightclub, ate his meal and left, telling the cashier that the
man who sat beside him at the counter (a total stranger) would cover the
check. A few weeks later, when he had a little money, Ruben returned and
asked to see Mr Basil. He was taken to the office and there he told Basil

Ruben Rivas

what he had done and gave him the two dollars he owed. Basil offered Ruben a job. Ruben asked for an audition instead. That night, between sets by the featured act, he sang. A man approached him and asked him if he had a manager. Ruben said no. It was Davy who introduced himself and asked Ruben to come to the Barclay Hotel the next day.

Ruben auditioned for my father in the Barclay's empty Club Indigo. Ruben played 'Granada'. Davy read the *Racing Form*. Ruben stopped mid-song. Davy asked him what was the matter. Ruben said, 'You're reading the *Racing Form*.' As Davy told it, he liked to see if the act was more interesting than the paper. Ruben was the only one who ever challenged him. Davy put the *Form* down and listened. When Ruben finished, they shook hands and Davy was Ruben's manager. With my father, a handshake was firmer than a dozen pages of boilerplate. In the world from which he had come, contracts were not written down, lest they turn up in some Crown attorney's evidence. So a man's handshake was his bond. You were a right guy, or you weren't. That handshake was the only contract Davy and Ruben ever had.

Over the next eight years, Ruben spent as much time with my father as he did with Mary, his wife, and my father spent as much time with Ruben as he did with us. Davy passed on to Ruben all the wisdom I was too young for. 'Only hire the best musicians,' he told him, 'the only screw-up you can afford to have in the band is you.' He told him, 'You want to get screwed, cash someone's cheque for him.' He told him to stay clear of Paul Volpe, the Toronto gangster who was later found murdered in the trunk of his wife's car. 'If he calls you over to his table,' Davy told Ruben, 'be polite, but don't take any favours and leave as soon you can.' And he advised Ruben to keep a 'fuck you' account, a bank account that no one else knew about, so 'if you ever have to, you can say "Fuck you, I don't need you."'

Ruben often chauffeured Davy around the city. (It was one of Davy's eccentricities that he never learned to drive.) One day they passed a small house for sale. Ruben, then an expectant father, admired it. 'Find out how much it costs,' Davy said. 'It doesn't matter,' Ruben told him, 'whatever it costs, I don't have it.' Still he checked, and reported to Davy that the down payment was $6,000. The next day, Davy pulled sixty one-hundred-dollar bills from his pocket and handed them to Ruben. Then my father added, 'But don't think this means you can ask me for money. Ask me for money, I'll tell you the same thing I tell everybody else, "Fuck off."'

THE ACT MY FATHER had managed before Ruben was the Canadaires. The group had been formed in the late 1940s by four teenagers from the St. Michael's Boys Choir School. Originally they called themselves the Otnorots (Toronto spelled backwards). By the early 1950s, two of them, Bernard Toorish and Connie Codarini, were ready to turn pro. The other two, John Perkins and Rudi Maugeri, stayed in school. Toorish and Codarini soon became two of the Four Lads, who recorded such 1950s hits as 'Istanbul (Not Constantinople)', 'Moments to Remember' and 'Standin' on the Corner Watchin' All the Girls Go By'. Perkins and Maugeri watched their old partners' success, and in 1952, decided to form their own quartet, the Canadaires.

Davy heard the Canadaires in 1953. He liked the act and, as later with Ruben Rivas, they shook hands. Davy booked the group here and there around Ontario and Quebec. Through old gambling associates, he scored a date for the boys on the Gene Carroll TV show in Cleveland. It meant an all-night, six-hundred-mile winter's drive from Sudbury to Cleveland in their 1939 Chevy with, according to legend, a broken heater. But it was American television.

'Get some haircuts,' Davy told them.

Gene Carroll liked the group and held them over. More importantly, he told the Cleveland disk jockey Bill Randle about them. Randle, 'The Pied Piper of Cleveland,' liked them as well and arranged an audition with Mercury Records, the Mob-financed, upstart Chicago record company. But, Randle told them, they needed a new name. Canadaires was hard to spell, meaningless to Americans, and too long for a marquee. The name he suggested, and the name they adopted, was the Crew-Cuts.

Mercury released the Crew-Cuts' first record, 'Crazy 'Bout You, Baby', in the spring of 1954. It was a hit. The boys quickly signed with an American manager and forgot about Davy. Mercury then handed the group the second song they were to record, a doo-wop number that had done well in the 'race' music market. The song was 'Sh-Boom'. The Crew-Cuts' version rose to Number One. 'Sh-Boom' was the first cross-over hit, the bridge between the smooth pop music of the 1950s and the emerging teenage craze, rock 'n' roll.

Several more hits followed, including 'Earth Angel' and 'Kokomo', but the Crew-Cuts' halcyon days were short-lived. Bill Randle had gone on to introduce Elvis Presley to northern audiences and, by 1957, rock 'n' roll ruled the air-waves. Teenagers now preferred the original, raunchier

Bill Randle, left, with Elvis Presley

versions of the songs the Crew-Cuts were cleaning up for Mercury. Still, the group toured the world for another seven years, numbering among their fans a fourteen-year-old who sought them out after a show in Liverpool. Paul McCartney would go on to form his own quartet with their own trademark haircuts. In his biography, McCartney credits the inspiration of the Crew-Cuts. 'He was a nice kid,' John Perkins remembered. 'We walked him home after the show.'

FINDING JOHN PERKINS a half-century after he left Toronto proved easier than I would have thought. Rudi Maugeri had died in 2004 and his obituary listed a brother, who was in the Toronto phone book. He directed me to Rudi's widow, who had John Perkins' email address.

I had one misgiving about contacting Perkins. In 1960, when the Crew-Cuts came back to Canada for a show, they were met by a process server. My father was suing them for breach of their handshake agreement.

The Crew-Cuts

Nothing came of the lawsuit, but I wondered how Perkins would feel when, fifty years later, he suddenly heard from Davy Bossin's heir. He wrote:

I am a bit surprised that you tracked me down here in Louisiana. Of course, I remember your father, who got us the early bookings that took us to Cleveland and the TV show that changed our lives. I also recall that he sued us when we returned to Toronto to play the Casino Theatre. It never went anywhere, but I do know that he was angry with us. He was probably right, but as young entertainers, we were being led by some people who had other than our interests at heart.

Perkins invited me to call him. When I did, he told me he did not remember Davy suggesting their haircuts. While he did recall the handshake, he thought the agreement was for an agent, not a manager.

'We would have been better off if he *was* our manager' Perkins said, going on to recount some of the bad decisions their managers made for them. In 1957, they gave up their rights to their Mercury hits, in return for being released from their contract. 'Don't worry, there will be more hits,' their manager told them, but there never were. In another misfire, the manager rejected the idea of a celebrity endorsement contract with a major haircare company. Instead he decided they would market their own Crew-Cuts hair gel. 'If you would like some,' Perkins told me, 'I have a garage full of the stuff.'

By 1964, the Crew-Cuts all had wives and children, and the performances were increasingly far-flung, so they packed it in. 'It was that or alimony,' Perkins said.

As our conversation was ending, John Perkins suddenly remembered another thing about Davy. 'I couldn't say for sure that your dad had anything to do with this, but I always wondered. Despite all our hits, except for one engagement at the Copa, the Crew-Cuts never played New York. I talked about it one time with a New York musician I knew, and he said "Yeah, the word around town is that the Crew-Cuts aren't right guys."'

I told Perkins about Davy's earlier career and connections, of which he knew nothing. But, I said, I couldn't picture Davy wielding that kind of power. It was afterwards that I recalled Ruben saying, 'If Davy Bossin said, "You don't work", you didn't work.' And it struck me that everything we know about our fathers amounts to a fraction of what we don't, and never will.

• • • 18. We may be related • • •

ONE DAY IN NOVEMBER, 2003, I received an email from an unfamiliar
sender, listed as 'Anagershon'.[1] The subject line read, 'We may be related.'
The text said only, 'The Gershons. Please send us an answer.' I puzzled
over Anagershon's message. I knew no Gershons. I did recall a family
friend whose name I remembered as Sam Gershwin—but it could have
been Gershon. When I was a little boy, it was Sam who had taught me how
to eat a sandwich without spilling its contents. I replied to Anagershon,
'Are you related to Sam? If so, please contact me.'

'Yes, this is us,' Anagershon replied by e-mail. 'I am Analena, widow of
Samuel Gershon. My english is very bad. Do you speak spanish or french?
My phone number is ...'

Analena had made several attempts to find me over the years and I had
harboured a faint hope of contacting her. I took a deep breath and dialled.

ANALENA GERSHON was born Analena de la Huerta Velàzquez, in 1936,
in Granada, Spain. The De la Huertas were an aristocratic family. Beautiful
and intelligent, Analena received a master's degree from the Universidad
Complutense de Madrid in 1963. As a graduation gift, Analena's parents
took her on a vacation on Majorca. They sailed from Valencia, and, that
night, in the ship's dining room, Analena noticed a handsome foreigner at
the next table. They exchanged smiles. He was much older than she was, and
she said to her mother, 'A man like that, I could marry tomorrow. I am tired
of these young idiots.' Her mother said, 'You are definitely crazy.'

Later that evening, on the deck, the man approached her and said in
formal, American-accented Spanish, '*Me parece que tienes frio*'—you appear
to be cold. He removed his jacket and placed it on her shoulders. They
talked for the rest of the evening. He gave her his card, which said 'Samuel
Gershon, import / export'. Observing Spanish proprieties, he did not ask
to contact her.

1 The names in this chapter are pseudonyms.

Bob, Sam and Marci, Madrid, 1962

The ship docked the next morning and, for the following week, Sam watched for the beautiful young woman he had met on the crossing. Finally, he spotted the De la Huertas at lunch in a café. He arranged for the manager to introduce him, and Señor de la Huerta invited Sam to join them. Sam and Analena courted for a month. Then he asked Sr de la Huerta for her hand. They married in May 1963. Analena moved to Madrid, into Sam's spacious apartment near the Museo del Prado. I had visited that apartment a year before, when I was sixteen.

SAM GERSHON was born in Chicago in 1919 and went to Europe with the American army in 1944. He landed at Normandy and fought in the Battle of the Bulge, where he was wounded. The army sent him back to the United States to convalesce in Florida. A handsome and personable man, Sam was reassigned as a recruiter.

After the war and an unsuccessful first marriage, Sam grew restive. He returned to Europe. While Analena was coming of age as a debutante, Sam enjoyed the moveable feast of expatriate life. Later, when Analena moved into Sam's apartment in Madrid, she would find souvenirs of her husband's bachelorhood: letters from a *chanteuse,* a lovingly autographed photograph of a dancer. She found a pair of panties, a diaphragm. 'It was a shock. I was very naive,' she recalled. Sam assured her that was all in his past.

A year went by. Analena was, by then, pregnant with their first child. Preparing a room as a nursery, she cleared out an old wardrobe and found, at the back, an easel, a box of oil paints, and an unfinished portrait of Sam. She also found a manila envelope of photographs of the artist, another beautiful woman. In some of the pictures, taken in different locales, she and Sam appeared together. In others, the woman was with a child. Leafing through the photos, Analena watched the baby grow into a boy. She knew in her bones it was Sam's son.

I was the boy.

Marci, my mother, met Sam Gershon in Florida in March 1945. She had come there for a winter holiday while Davy stayed in Toronto. Marci and Davy had been married six years by then, and the marriage had become strained. 'Your father never should have married,' my mother told me once. 'He was really a man's man. He didn't know how to be around women. I think he was afraid of them. Don't get me wrong, he was a good man and a good husband. After you came along, he was a good father. But he never talked to me. He didn't know how. And he absolutely refused to have children. I wanted a family.'

The day Marci arrived in Miami, she met Sam at the hotel pool. He was younger than she was by seven years, but he was easy to talk to, solicitous and sympathetic. They fell in love quickly. Their love-making was, for Marci, a revelation. Where Davy was reserved, Sam was passionate and attentive. As the days went by, Marci felt more and more torn. Sam's solution was simple. 'Leave him,' he told her. 'We'll have as many children as you want.' Marci left Florida in turmoil.

The night she got back to Toronto was, according to my mother, the night I was conceived. Marci talked about the circumstances differently at different times. (Consistency was never a hallmark of Marci's conversation.) In one version she just let nature take its course. In another, she tricked Davy, pretending her diaphragm was in place. 'The fact is, I had learned a thing or two from Sam,' she told me. 'Your father didn't know what hit him.' Marci never said anything to me to indicate that I might have been Sam's child.

When Marci told Davy she was pregnant, he blew up. He told her he would arrange an abortion. Marci refused. If she insisted on having the baby, Davy answered, he would leave. 'No, you won't,' she told him. 'You will stay here until the baby is born. After that, you can do what you want.' According to Marci, Davy remained adamant throughout her pregnancy,

Sam and Marci, 1945

but when he saw me, it was love at first sight; I held on to his finger, and his resistance melted. This may have actually happened. With Marci you could never tell when beauty trumped truth, or when something she wanted to be the case became so in the telling. In any event, Davy did not leave, then or for the rest of his life.

Once I was born, Marci's path was clear. She stayed with Davy. She maintained her friendship with Sam and he became a friend of the family. She visited him from time to time in Chicago or Miami, sometimes with me. Later, she would see him in Europe. I believe—no, I am sure—Marci and Sam remained lovers.

The night before his wedding—Sam's first wedding, in 1947—Sam telephoned Marci from Chicago. He told her, tearfully, he would still call it off and marry her, if she would have him. Marci told him it was just nerves; he was sweet and probably drunk. She told him she loved him, but he should get some sleep, get up early, and get married.

WHEN ANALENA FOUND the portrait of Sam, the story he told her was different from the one Marci told me. Yes, Marci had been one of his lovers. She thought that the child she was carrying was his, but he didn't believe it, and when he met me, as he had several times, he was certain that I was not his child. Analena did not know what to think. However, with time, marriage and family, her concern dimmed.

The question did not arise again until some years after Sam's death in 1978. One day Analena was visiting a friend whose wife had been my mother's friend and confidante on her trips to Europe. 'Of course the boy was Sam's,' the man told her. 'We all knew.' The widower was a judge and a man of absolute honour, Analena assured me, and his certainty rekindled her intuition. Her daughters, she believed, had a Canadian half-brother.

Sometime in the mid-1990s, Analena decided to contact Marci. She called information in various Canadian cities. In Toronto there was a listing for M. Bossin. Analena called the number, and Marci picked up the phone. By then my mother was in her eighties and her peculiar, crooked way with a story was becoming more pronounced, mixing with the early stages of the dementia she would experience in her last years. Marci told me later that she had trouble understanding Analena. For some reason, she said, the woman who had called seemed to want her daughter to meet me. Marci explained to her that I was married and had a family.

I can only guess what Marci was thinking during that phone call. Her

confusion may have been just as she described it. On the other hand, Analena may have opened a door that my mother had kept locked for forty years. If so, it would have been characteristic of her to lead her unwanted caller on a wild goose chase.

At her end of the line, Analena found the conversation disjointed and difficult. She did not leave her number and never called back. It would be another half-dozen years before she tried to find me again, via the internet.

When Analena and I finally spoke in 2003, we put together what each of us knew. We discussed the possibility of DNA testing. I suggested I test with my cousin John to see if he and I shared Bossin genes. As it turns out, DNA testing is not that simple. The only way to ascertain if Sam was my biological father was to compare my DNA with Analena's daughters'. It would cost several thousand dollars, and the tests would only indicate probability. Further analysis, for several thousand dollars more, could reveal additional indicators, but even then, there was no such thing as a definitive second-generation match. I emailed what I had found out to Analena, but did not hear back. I left her several more messages, which went unanswered. Years slipped by. Recently I tried to reach her again, with no success. I did manage to locate one of her daughters and left a message. I got a polite but firm response. She did not wish to communicate with me. However, at my request, she sent me a photograph of Marci's portrait of Sam.

I never tested my DNA, and I am only mildly curious about what the results might reveal. The fact is, Davy was my father. Sam taught me to eat a sandwich, but it was Davy who taught me not to bet with anyone who offered to make the jack of spades spit cider in my ear. It was Davy who played catch with me, who tucked me in, read me *Uncle Remus*, and explained that one man's laughing place isn't necessarily another's. Davy taught me, 'Fish don't get caught, if they keep their mouth shut.' He taught me that men in authority are likely to be liars and scoundrels. He taught me to know who is a right guy, and to be one myself. And it was on Davy's knee, or beside him at Maple Leaf Stadium, or tucked between him and his cronies at a delicatessen, that I learned that nothing beats a good story. No question about it, I am Davy's son.

DAVY KNEW SAM and, if he suspected anything, he did not let on. One time in the late 1940s, Davy was in Chicago on layoff business. He had a pair of tickets to *Oklahoma!*, the hot show in the city. Davy intended to

take a cousin, but the cousin cancelled. Davy called Marci, home with me in Toronto, and asked if she could think of anyone to take to the show. She suggested Sam. Davy called him. Sam accepted the invitation reluctantly. Before he set out, he put his service revolver in his jacket pocket. Davy loved the show, but Sam seemed distracted. Afterwards, he invited Sam out for a bite. Sam knew that if Davy or his underworld associates planned to teach him a lesson, it would not be at a crowded theatre, it would be after. He declined. So Davy said goodnight, and told Sam it was good to see him. Sam hailed a cab, feeling foolish but relieved.

What intrigues me about Sam's place in my family's history is not what it says about me, but what it says about Marci and Davy. Marci was never apologetic about Sam. 'You have to live, Bobby,' she once told me. 'It isn't easy. You do the best you can by other people, but you have to take care of yourself too.' She was sure Davy never knew Sam was her lover. 'Your father said to me "Marci, there are good girls and bad girls, and you are the good kind. That's all there is to that."'

I believe that my mother knew, or believed, or came to believe, that I was conceived on the night she returned to Toronto from Miami in April 1945. My gut, and my daughter's resemblance to her cousins, tell me that is how it went. But Marci also believed that Davy did not know about Sam and her.

Sure.

Davy, Bob, Sam and Marci. Miami, 1950.

Davy

Sam

Bob

• • • 20. Heaven • • •

ON FRIDAY, April 19, 1963, my father left home for the last time. That morning Ruben Rivas, the bandleader Davy managed, picked him up at our house, and drove the two of them downtown to the Embassy, a new night-club in the city. Ruben's band was booked to open the club a few weeks hence and they were meeting with the manager to negotiate the final details of the contract. Shortly after they sat down, my father complained of heartburn. He broke out in a sweat. Then he pissed himself. 'Jesus, Davy,' Ruben said, 'I better take you to the hospital.' 'No hospital,' my father said, slurring the words. Davy pitched forward, unconscious. Ruben caught him and held him while the manager called an ambulance. Davy had had a cerebral hemorrhage. He never regained consciousness and died two days later. He was fifty-eight. I was seventeen.

At one point in the next few chaotic days, I asked my mother if Dad had left any instructions about his funeral or about what he wanted done with his remains. She didn't say anything at first. Then, for the first time since Davy's death, she smiled, or half-smiled. She said, 'He said to scatter his ashes on the race-track.' We didn't do it. Instead, we buried him in half of a double plot in the Holy Blossom Memorial Park on the outskirts of Toronto. He was buried on April 24, 1963. It snowed.

It would be another forty-five years before Marci joined Davy in her half of the plot. She never remarried. 'I can have a man in my bed when I want to,' she said. 'Why should I do his laundry?'

MANY WHO KNEW DAVY thought we would be left wealthy, but that was not the case. We had always lived comfortably and modestly in the small house Davy had bought, at Marci's insistence, when I was a year old. He paid $9,000 for it, purchasing it outright with cash, the way he paid for everything. We never moved after that, nor felt the need to. Marci lived there until she was ninety-two.

Those who thought Davy wealthy must have thought him eccentric or miserly, but the fact is, his comfort and ours did not depend on new clothes, a new car, or other things that cost a lot of money. Marci explained

this to friends and family who were concerned for us. Still, Davy's brothers remained convinced there was a stash of money somewhere. My uncle Hye went to the United States and sought out Frank Costello and other old colleagues of Davy's, but he came back empty-handed. If Davy kept a 'fuck you' account, we never found it.

So Marci went to work, cobbling together an income. She got commissions for paintings, she modelled, and she worked as a publicist for her brother's safety equipment company. There she wrote press releases for new products. 'I thought, if I can understand how they work, then anyone can, and that is how I wrote them up.' Safe in our small but un-mortgaged house, Marci and I got by, and quietly thrived. Crime, you might say, if handled with discretion and moderation, paid.

SO DID GAMBLING, at least for its purveyors, and eventually the Ontario Government, once so relentless in its pursuit of my father, took its own seat at the table. From where we are today, it is hard to fathom the authorities' fixation on Davy and the racing news he provided every day at two o'clock. These days, Ontario looks to Davy's sin to fund basic government programs. The gaming industry, as gambling has been genteelly rebranded, has been, effectively, nationalized. The numbers racket, the carpet joint and the horse room are now the provincial lottery, the licensed casino and the off-track betting office. Across the country, governments not only tolerate gambling, they encourage it. Public funds finance promotional campaigns that would dumbfound Abe Orpen or Frank Costello. 'Imagine the freedom,' 'Don't think for an instant,' 'I won $21,000 while washing the dishes!' exclaim ads for provincial lotteries.

'Human beings is gamble-minded,' Frank Costello once said, and it is certainly true in Canada. By 1950, four out of five Canadians told pollsters that they had gambled in some form. By 1995, Manitobans were spending more money on government-licensed gambling than on groceries. In 2000, in economically depressed Sydney, Nova Scotia, the town's casino took over 50 million dollars out of the troubled local economy.

But gamble-minded as we are and have always been, it took nearly a century for Canadian legislators to stop pretending that we were not. Only in 1969 did the door open, a crack, to bingo parlours, casinos, betting offices and lottery kiosks. The Criminal Law Amendment Act of 1969, which also softened the laws against contraception, abortion and homosexuality, faced vehement opposition and even a filibuster, but in the end, the

Criminal Code was liberalized, at least a little, by the first Canadian Prime Minister who had not grown up in the Victorian or Edwardian age, Pierre Trudeau.

Bookmaking, however, stayed a crime and it remains so to this day.

IT TOOK ONTARIO another half-dozen years to turn gambling to its advantage, but in 1975, the province instituted its Wintario lottery. It was another twenty years before Ontario opened its first legal casino. The decision was taken by the province's first and, so far, only NDP government. Ironically, the slightly socialist New Democratic Party was the direct descendant of the social gospel movement, which had been among gambling's staunchest foes. The irony was not lost on Ontario's new young premier, Bob Rae, who told his colleagues during cabinet discussions of the casino project, 'This is like the United Church discussing how best to run a whorehouse.'

Rae's young cabinet possessed little of the old Upper-Canadian moral abhorrence for gambling (although one NDP parliamentarian resigned from the caucus over the casino decision). The public felt the same. Rae's office received more pro-casino calls than objections. In fact the gravest reservations came from the existing gambling interests. Rae appeased them. Those who relied on church bingos and charity Monte Carlo nights demanded, and got, liberalized rules; negotiations began immediately with native bands for casinos on reserves; and the horse-racing industry was promised a fat share of the proceeds from licensed off-track betting.

Had you been walking through Holy Blossom Memorial Park at the time and heard a faint howling, it might have been the wind or it might have been Davy laughing.

LOSING MY FATHER when I was a teenager was a blow, but I knew even then that you play the cards you are dealt. I suppose Davy taught me that. My cousin John says I never cried, which he thought was unnatural. I don't know if it was natural or not—and I did cry a little, in private—it just seemed to me like the best way to handle it. I'm not much for grief, then or since. But I have often wished I could trade some of the time I had with Davy as a boy, for time together man to man. There are so many things we never talked about. We never, for instance, spoke of love, or sex, or marriage. Though I did hear something of his views, second-hand.

In the late 1950s, Ruben and Mary Rivas's marriage was in trouble. I

suspect chorus girls were involved. 'Davy was such an unusual man,' Mary told me, recalling that time. 'For the most part he was so gruff. He really was a forbidding character. But when he wanted to be—and when he talked to me about this, you could have knocked me over with a feather—he was very thoughtful. He told me, if you love someone, if you really love them, you have to love them the way they are. He didn't say he was talking about your mother and her, well, you know, but I knew that was what he was telling me. He really helped me. Davy, of all people.'

Davy was full of contradictions, as we all are. 'He had nerves of steel,' one of his old friends told me. Yet he never learned to drive, never learned to swim and, so far as I know, never set foot on an airplane. On the other hand, there was the time his friend Bill Gold drove them to Cleveland for the 1948 World Series. The afternoon they arrived, Davy said he had some people to meet and invited Gold along. They took a cab to a local gambling club, where they were shown to the back room. The meeting turned out to be with Charlie and Rocco Fischetti, the leaders of the Capone Mob. (Capone had died the year before.) Gold could not get away fast enough. He made an excuse and told Davy he would see him back at the hotel. 'I'll get someone to drive you,' Charlie Fischetti told Gold, 'just wait in the Caddy out back.' Gold did, and while he waited, he checked the glove box. It contained several guns and a large supply of bullets. He closed it again, got out of the car and hailed a cab. The next morning the Cleveland papers headlined a gangland shooting in the club where Davy had spent the afternoon.

Unlike Bill Gold, Davy had been in his element that afternoon, sitting around shooting the breeze with guys who knew what was what. According to their biographers, Frank Costello and Meyer Lansky were much the same: they liked nothing better than *shmoozing* with pals, telling stories. After work, gangsters often enjoyed simple pleasures. One journalist tells of a time he came upon some of the biggest names in organized crime gathered by the pool at a Miami hotel. They were engrossed in a poker game. The stakes? Dimes. Davy and his friends were like that. For them, nothing beat a leisurely evening together in the bleachers at Maple Leaf Stadium, cooled by the breeze, swapping stories.

I mentioned earlier that Davy did not tell jokes, except for two, one already reported. The other he told on one of those nights at the ballpark. One of Davy's pals, Sack Sniderman, had recently passed away. His friends were, in their way, sitting *shiva*, their sadness expressed in wisecracking

recollections of their friend's eccentricities. They told stories of Sack's milkman days, shook their heads over his crazy betting system, and speculated on how he was faring at the ethereal windows of Elysian Park. As usual, Davy did not contribute to the banter, preferring his newspaper. But when someone called on him, he folded the paper and told the story of Benny Bermuda's arrival in Heaven.

When Benny got there, there was a big crowd outside the gate, so Benny took a place on a bench to wait his turn. Eventually, his name was called and he approached St. Peter, who looked up from a large ledger. 'Are you Benjamin Bermuda, the horse player?' Peter asked. Benny nodded. Peter gave him a baleful look and said, 'I'm sorry, Mr Bermuda, I just don't have a place for you. My horse-player card is filled right up.'

Benny went back to the bench and sat down to think about his situation. Then he had an idea. He went back to St. Peter and said, 'Let me ask you something. Have you got Johnny McBride in there?' Peter checked the ledger and said he did. 'How about Ginger James? T.G. Whelon? Canada Bill Jones?' Peter affirmed them all. 'Well,' Benny said, 'those boys and me go back a long way. Would you mind taking them a message for me?'

Peter said he would.

'Good,' Benny said, perking up. 'Tell them Bermuda says there's a filly in the sixth at Pimlico named Calgary Girl, who's gonna run a hole in the wind, and none of those east-coast punters know it, because she's done all her racing in the bull rings out west. She's on the board at 30 to 1.' He gave St Peter a wink. 'Tell the boys *that*.'

Peter arched an eyebrow, but went off to deliver the message. Pretty soon, here comes McBride and Jones and James and the rest, streaming out of the Pearly Gates, hailing the first cloud for Baltimore.

'Well, Mr Bermuda,' St. Peter said, 'I guess there's room for you now. Come on in.'

Benny started for the gate, but then he shied. 'You know,' he said, 'there just might be something to that filly after all. Hey, Ginger, Johnny, Bill, wait for me!'

EVERYONE in our section of the bleachers laughed, and Davy, as he always did, laughed as hard as any of them.

• Afterword, Sources and Acknowledgements •

CALLING THIS BOOK a memoir was the publisher's idea. Fair enough; books have to be categorized, and 'storybook' wasn't one of the options.[1] But that is how I think of it: this is the story I might tell you on a summer night in the bleachers if I really got wound up. I suppose it is a memoir of sorts. But my father died when I was just a teen, so my personal memories of him end early. Of necessity, I have reconstructed much of *Davy the Punk* from what others told me, and from documents my father had nothing to do with. That part of the story is interesting too, at least I think it is, so I will tell it here, and, in the process, thank the people without whose help this book would have been slim indeed.

I did get some of the story straight from the horse's mouth, from my father. Among friends and family, Davy was neither secretive nor defensive about his past, and I liked nothing better than listening in when he told his stories. I only wish that I had asked him more questions, and that I had a better memory than I do. Of course, in the end, our fathers' lives always remain a mystery, and mine no less despite my best efforts to snoop. Over the years I have learned a lot about what Davy did, but how he did it, I can only guess. I know, for instance, that he went to New York around 1950 to tell Frank Costello he was quitting the gambling business. But how did he feel boarding the train—worried? confident? nonchalant? Or there is Bill Gold's story of Davy happily kibitzing with the murderous Fischetti brothers in a Cleveland club in 1948. Was Davy really as relaxed as his friend remembered a half-century later, when he was ninety-two? I decided to take Gold's word and have reported the story that way. The book is peppered with choices like that. My father is the subject of *Davy the Punk*, and I have portrayed him as

1 As well as this book, I have written a stage version of my father's story, a one-man musical called *Songs and Stories of Davy the Punk*. If you are interested in it, please visit www.davythepunk.com. If you would like to catch a performance, or if you would like to contact me about anything at all, I can be reached at: bob@bossin.com

accurately as a story-teller can but, in the end, while it is his life, it is my story.

I think Davy would understand that, having been a consummate story-teller himself. I heard that with my own ears. His love of a good story got bred in my bones. Without that hand-me-down passion, I would never have kept after Davy the Punk through all the obstacles and dead-ends inherent in chasing a man with a fifty-year head-start.

My mother was another important source. She outlived my father by forty-six years and she answered my many prying questions with equanimity and remarkable candour. Her only condition was that I not publish what she told me until after she died. (She died in 2006.)

After my mother and father I am, in a way, most indebted to my old housemate Joe Medjuck and to Alex Haley, the author of *Roots*. Sometime in the late 1970s Joe heard an interview in which Haley called on everyone with a tape recorder to go out and tape their family elders' stories. The moment Joe told me about it, I committed to doing just that. My only hesitation was that neither my relatives nor the Bossin family story were very interesting. I quickly discovered I was wrong on both counts. Over the years, I recorded interviews with a dozen aunts, uncles and cousins, filling many a cassette. I always asked them about Davy.

Making those tapes, I found that I liked interviewing people. So I began to seek out my father's surviving friends and cronies. Some clammed up, but others provided lively and revealing accounts, among them Alex Barris, Dave Broadfoot, Tom DeJourno, Bill Gold, Paul

Grosney, Joey Hollingsworth and Ruben and Mary Rivas. Emboldened, I cast the net wider and interviewed David Humphrey, by then a retired judge (and also, he hinted without quite confessing, the anonymous fan who tripped Ray 'Bibbles' Bawel as he ran down the sideline during the 1957 Grey Cup game). I talked with Jocko Thomas, then in his nineties, about his many years as the *Toronto Star*'s police reporter. Jocko directed me to former Toronto Police Staff Sergeant Herb Thurston. And so on.

Those conversations were spread over a decade while I went about the rest of my life. As the century closed, I turned in earnest to Davy's story, only to find the trail had gone cold. Most of his contemporaries had died. Court records proved scanty. A fire had destroyed Toronto's old police files. But a freedom-of-information request hit pay dirt. Buried in the archived papers of the Office of the Attorney General of Ontario was a file labelled 'David Bossin vs Bell Telephone Company'. It was an inch thick and filled with correspondence, memos and reports from the 1940s.

In another stroke of luck, I discovered that in 1951, the Ontario government had empanelled a Select Committee on the Administration of Justice, chaired by Dana Porter. (Porter would later become Chief Justice of the Ontario Court of Appeal and rule that *Fanny Hill* was fit to be read by Ontarians.) That was the time when the Kefauver hearings were in full swing in the U.S. and the authorities on both sides of the border were convinced that the race wire was the root of all evil, or at least evil's Achilles' heel. Accordingly, one of the hot topics for the Porter Committee was how Davy Bossin got away. I flew to Toronto from British Columbia where I had moved in 1980, and settled into a carrel at the old Ontario Archives building. There I leafed through a thousand pages of testimony. Hundreds of those pages were devoted to the Crown's failure to put Davy out of business. Photocopying archival material was prohibitively expensive in those days, so I sat in my carrel, whispering the text into my trusty cassette recorder.

Alas, one document eluded me: I could find no record of Davy's hearing before the Transport Board. Thomas Agar, my father's lawyer, had died years before, leaving his files to a partner who had subsequently died too. No help there. I could find no Agar relatives, and no institutional recollection of the proceedings. But then, on the last morning I was in Toronto, the Archives called. They had found a box of documents submitted to the Porter Committee. I had just enough time to get there and rummage through the box before catching my plane—and there it was, a

yellowing carbon copy of the transcript of Davy's Transport Board hearing. (The box also contained the photo that appears on the cover of this book. It was taken by a police photographer during a raid on 16 Royal York Road in 1942.) I was sorely tempted to tuck the transcript into my backpack. Security at the archives was lax and surely no one but me had any interest in it. But my better angels prevailed and I returned the transcript to its box, duly noting the call number. Nearly a decade later, when I next returned (life having intervened again) there was the transcript. By then I had a digital camera, and I shot each page.

Another thing that had come along in the intervening years was the internet. Suddenly every paper ever published by the *Toronto Star* or the *Globe and Mail* was on line and searchable. I typed in 'Bossin', and as if by magic, conjured up Doug McQuarrie's 1938 retelling of Davy's Big Chocolate story. When I searched 1940, up came Gordon Sinclair's live coverage of the raid on the *Canadian Turf and Sports Bulletin*. Other online incantations summoned the transcripts of the public sessions of the Kefauver hearings. Google Images offered me photos of everyone from Senator Charles Tobey to, well, Virgina Hill.

Not everything from those pre-computer days has been digitized, but what hasn't been can often be obtained through the remarkable network of inter-university-library loans. I am indebted to University of British Columbia Professor Emeritus Richard Pollay for his help in navigating this sea of information. If I could name it, Rick could help me get a peek at it, whether it was the last surviving copy of the memoir of 1940s wire-tapper Cheesebox Callahan (located in a library stack in Texas) or a 1949 PhD thesis entitled *Gambling and the Social Structure: A Sociological Study of Lotteries and Horse Racing in Contemporary America.* The author of the latter, Edward Devereux, it turned out, had carried out 'a fair bit of field work, mostly on the organization of book making and the wire service' in Toronto around 1940. Could he have sat in the office of the *Canadian Turf and Sports Bulletin* listening to Davy tell stories?

The books, articles and theses I read number in the hundreds. I am indebted to abebooks.com (another godsend of the internet age), the Vancouver Island Regional Library, the Vancouver Public Library (with particular thanks to Heather Gale), the Toronto Public Library (thanks to Jill Shefrin) and the Koerner Library at the University of British Columbia.

Many of the institutions whose resources I used are being squeezed by under-funding, down-sizing or privatization. Their ability to collect

and retain material, and to facilitate the kind of research that went into this book is being undercut. Thereby our history slips from our grasp. The devaluation of archives and libraries (and of paper and books) is one of the sad, short-sighted failings of these penny-pinching times.

RAISING *Davy the Punk* has taken a whole village, as the saying goes. Were I to thank everyone who aided and abetted me along the way, the list would run to pages. I won't do that, but I am grateful to my many unnamed friends and helpers. I hope they are proud of the end product of all our efforts.

That said, I do want to thank a short list of people whose contributions were essential: Tim Inkster and The Porcupine's Quill, who saw the merit in this project when other publishers did not; the Canada Council who saw it too; my editor, Doris Cowan; Peter Froehlich, dramaturge or, in this case, book-a-turge; my cousin and chief Bossin-family historian, Shayndel Tallan; my longtime comrade and sometime manager, Gary Cristall; the aforementioned Rick Pollay and the Acme Delivery Company; my neighbour and go-to gal for anything to do with publishing, Ingrid Witvoet; Rose Marie 'Hawkeye' Harrop; my ex, Mary Jo Fulmer; and Simon Webb, the director of the stage version of *Davy the Punk*. Above all, I want to thank my partner, Elizabeth Shefrin. In this, as in everything else, I have depended on her counsel, creativity and sense of humour.

I HAVE A CONFESSION to make. My father's in-house campaign against gambling worked. I don't gamble—playing stud poker is not gambling, as any poker-player worth his salt will tell you—and, truth to tell, I have never had much interest in horse racing. Nearly everything I know about racing, beyond Davy's stories, comes from books. So does most of what I know about the Mafia, about old Toronto, and about the history of anti-Semitism in Canada. All from good old books. The bibliography that follows lists some great old books, at least I think so. Read enough books about anything and some of them are going to display timeless writing. So it was lovely to rediscover, for instance, what a first-class story-teller Peter Gzowski was. Or to stumble across Joe H. Palmer's immaculate turf reporting. Seeing the Mafia through the myth-busting lens of Robert Lacey or Gay Talese, or feeling the full power of scholarship in the work of Abella and Troper or Petrovsky-Shtern—these are some of the rewards offered by the books listed on the following page.

Irving Abella, Harold Troper. *None Is Too Many: Canada And The Jews of Europe 1933–1948*. Lester and Orpen Dennys, 1982.

Lita-Rose Betcherman. *The Little Band: The clashes between the Communists and the political and legal establishment in Canada, 1928–1932.* Deneau, 1982.

——. *The Swastika and the Maple Leaf, Fascist Movements in Canada in the Thirties.* Fitzhenry & Whiteside, 1975.

Peter Gzowski. *An Unbroken Line.* McClelland and Stewart, 1983.

Laura Hillenbrand. *Seabiscuit, An American legend.* Ballantine, 2002.

Leo Katcher. *The Big Bankroll: The Life and Times of Arnold Rothstein.* Arlington House, 1958.

Leonard Katz. *Uncle Frank: The Biography of Frank Costello.* Drake, 1973.

Robert Lacey. *Little Man: Meyer Lansky and the Gangster Life.* Little, Brown, 1991.

Cyril Levitt and William Shaffir. *The Riot at Christie Pits.* Lester & Orpen Dennys, 1987.

Sammy Luftspring with Brian Swarbrick. *Call Me Sammy.* Prentice-Hall, 1975.

Suzanne Morton. *At Odds: Gambling and Canadians 1919–1969.* University of Toronto Press, 2003.

Joe H. Palmer. *This Was Racing.* A.S. Barnes and Co., 1953.

Yohana Petrovsky-Shtern. *Jews in the Russian Army, 1827–1917.* Cambridge University Press, 2008.

Damon Runyon. *Guys and Dolls and Other Stories.* Penguin, 1956.

David G. Schwartz, *Cutting the Wire: Gambling, Prohibition and the Internet.* University of Nevada Press, 2005.

Jane Smiley. *Horse Heaven.* Knopf, 2000.

Gay Talese. *Honor Thy Father.* World Publishing, 1971.

Jocko Thomas. *From Police Headquarters: True Tales from the Big City Crime Beat.* Stoddart, 1982.

William Weintraub. *City Unique: Montreal Days And Nights in the 1940s and '50s.* McClelland & Stewart, 1998.

• The Photographs •

MOST OF THE PHOTOGRAPHS in this book are 50 to 100 years old. Many are from my mother's collection, or from the photo albums of other members of the extended Bossin family. (I have not included our family photos in the list below.) I am particularly indebted to our unofficial family-photo archivist, David Tallan.

The 'public' photos in the book come from a variety of archives and libraries. (Once again, I want to acknowledge the important work of archivists.) Occasionally, they are from private collections. I have done my best to find out who took the photos and, if they are not in the public domain, who holds the copyright. This is rarely easy so long after the fact. If I have inadvertently given short shrift to an aged photographer, or to his or her heirs, I apologize.

Since this is not a formal history book, I have not included detailed citations for each archival photograph. Nowadays, the filing numbers can easily be ascertained by searching the on-line catalogue of the archive holding the photograph. Usually, the staff are helpful and good-natured. Or you can contact me. I have been in your shoes.

— BB

SOURCES AND CREDITS

The photograph on the front cover is courtesy of the Archives of Ontario.

p. 9 – Maple Leaf Stadium. Courtesy of the City of Toronto Archives.

p. 16 – Scotty Craigmyle. Courtesy of the Craigmyle family.

p. 19 – Paul Grosney. Courtesy of the Grosney family.

p. 23 – Jewish Newsboys, c. 1910. Courtesy of the Ontario Jewish Archives.

p. 32 – The Ward, 'Slum courtyard, 142 Agnes Street'. Courtesy of the City of Toronto Archives.

p. 32 – The Ward, 'Slums, rear 21 Elizabeth Street'. Courtesy of the City of Toronto Archives.

p. 37 – Abram Orpen. Courtesy of the City of Toronto Archives.

p. 54 – Morris Fishman. Courtesy of the Canadian Horse Racing Hall of Fame. Thanks to Louis Cauz.

p. 73 – United Bakers Dairy Restaurant. Courtesy of the Ladovsky family.

p. 76 – Moses Annenberg. Courtesy of the Historical Society of Pennsylvania.

p. 80 – Waxey Gordon. *New York World-Telegram, 1933*. Collection of the Library of Congress.

p. 80 – Frank Nitti. *New York World-Telegram*. Collection of the Library of Congress.

p. 104 – Gordon Sinclair. *The Toronto Star*. City of Toronto Archives.

p. 109 – Frank Costello. *New York World-Telegram, 1951*. Collection of the Library of Congress.

p. 116 – 'Mayor LaGuardia smashes confiscated slot machines, Oct. 6, 1936'. *New York World-Telegram*. Courtesy of the LaGuardia and Wagner Archives.

p. 120 – Estes Kefauver. Courtesy of Tennessee State Library and Archives.

p. 122 – Virginia Hill. Collection of the Library of Congress.

p. 122 – Senator Charles Tobey. Collection of the Library of Congress.

p. 129 – 16 Royal York Road. Courtesy of the Archives of Ontario.

p. 144 – Gangy Cohen (aka Jack Gordon) in *Golden Boy*. Courtesy of Columbia Pictures.

p. 154 – Ruben Rivas. Courtesy of the Rivas family.

p. 157 – Bill Randle and Elvis Presley. Also pictured are Tommy Edwards, and Bill Black. Courtesy of Chris Kennedy.

p. 158 – The Crew-Cuts. Courtesy of John Perkins.

The photograph on the back cover is by Barry Price.

BORN IN TORONTO in 1946, Bob Bossin has spent forty years writing and performing music and stories, most notably as the founder (with Marie-Lynn Hammond) of the legendary Canadian folk group, Stringband. Called 'funny, informative and inspiring at the same time' by Pete Seeger, Bossin has recorded a dozen albums, performed all over the world and added a number of songs to the Canadian folk canon. He has also written books, plays, essays, articles and, once upon a time, poetry. Concurrent with the release of *Davy the Punk*, Bossin will be touring a live one-man musical about his father. He lives on Gabriola Island, B.C., with his son, Davy, and his partner, visual artist Sima Elizabeth Shefrin.

A NOTE ABOUT THE TYPE. 'Rimmer Pro' was the last font completed by the Canadian type designer, illustrator and letterpress printer Jim Rimmer before his passing in early 2010. Jim Rimmer was born in 1934 in Vancouver, and was noted in later years as the proprietor of the Pie Tree Press of New Westminster, for which he designed many typefaces in metal including Hannibal, made especially for his limited edition of *Tom Sawyer*.

'Rimmer Pro' was originally to be called Doubloon and was intended for use in a planned limited edition of *Treasure Island* (coincidentally one of Bob Bossin's all-time favourite books).